Re-Covering in God

40 Days Wrestling with God

SUE WATLOV PHILLIPS

WESTBOW·
PRESS
A DIVISION OF THOMAS NELSON
& ZONDERVAN

Revised Standard Version of the Bible, copyright 1952 [2nd edition, 1971] by the Division of Christian Education of the National Council of the Churches of Christ in the United States of America. Used by permission. All rights reserved.

WestBow Press books may be ordered through booksellers or by contacting:

WestBow Press
A Division of Thomas Nelson & Zondervan
1663 Liberty Drive
Bloomington, IN 47403
www.westbowpress.com
1 (866) 928-1240

ISBN: 978-1-4908-2292-1 (sc)
ISBN: 978-1-4908-2291-4 (hc)
ISBN: 978-1-4908-2293-8 (e)

Library of Congress Control Number: 2014900732

Printed in the United States of America.

WestBow Press rev. date: 05/09/2014

This is devotional is dedicated to God,

Mom and Dad,

Pamela Sue Wynn,

and all people
suffering with the disease of alcoholism,
chemical health issues, or other —isms.

. . . The Lord has forsaken me,
    my Lord has forgotten me."
"Can a woman forget her sucking child,
    that she has no compassion the son of her womb?
Even these may forget,
    yet I will never forget you.
Behold, I have graven you into the palms of my hands.
                                    Isaiah 49:14-16

Gratitude

I thank God for His love, refuge, faith, patience, long-suffering, guidance, hope, and peace. I was lost in alcoholism and prescribed medications, but God allowed me to survive and now thrive.

I thank Pamela Sue Wynn who mentored, argued, guided, and dialogued with me in writing this devotional. Her patience, guidance, encouragement, support and prayers helped bring it to fruition.

I owe many thanks to my family who compassionately struggled with me as I accepted my disease of alcoholism over the last few years, especially my Dad and Mom, brother and sisters, Uncle Red, Bernice, Aunt Peggy, my cousin Ginger and Delores P.

I am indebted to my dear friends who supported me in court and visited me in treatment and jail—Elaine R. and family, Janet P., Ruth and Rod T., AA sponsors, and friends; to my friends and prayer warriors Kathy R., Jean, Katie, Julie and Dale M., Patricia M., Elinor and Wilbur W. and family, Tom and Lori, Pastors Becky, Jim, Dan, Gary D., and John; to Sherri D, Becky F., Denise S., Lori and Tom B., Tom and Betty M. and family members, Anita B., Glorin P., Michael S., Tedd and Patty B., Pam T., David M., Patricia M., Lou and Larry T. To Elim, Sand Lake Alliance, Pequot Lakes Baptist Churches prayer chains, Edgewood Vista Bible study group, and MICAH Board and staff, and many others.

Thank you to the patients in treatment settings, AA groups, and people I served time with in jail who helped me learn more about the devastating impact of this disease, for their persistence, hope, faith, love, and service; and to treatment staff and doctors for their compassion, patience, firmness, and love, especially Cecelia, JoAnn, Andrea, and Diane; and to the compassion of the court and those I hurt who gave me another chance in life, and hopefully forgive me.

Introduction

"Don't let anything steal your joy." Alcohol stole my joy.

I began drinking at about age twenty-five, after a quarter of a century of having nothing to do with alcohol or drugs as a Christian growing up in the Baptist tradition, and as I trained as an athlete. In my late teens and early twenties, I rejected the legalistic and exclusivity of organized religion, as I had come to believe, and still do, that Jesus taught that the commandments and prophets are fulfilled when I love God with all my heart, soul, mind and strength, and that I love others as myself.

During my teenage years in the 1960s, I became actively involved in several social justice issues: Civil Rights, women's athletics, women's rights, and Vietnam War protests. I also began volunteering and helping other youth struggling at home or running away from home. I felt strongly called by my faith to social justice and service to others. As I continued to train, hoping to go to the Olympics in track, I was constantly torn between a very self-focused training in sports and my faith's call to social justice. I worked professionally with youth in shelters and residential settings during my late teens and early twenties, while I trained and competed.

I was devastated when injured in sports in my early twenties. The knee injury was misdiagnosed by a sport physician without experience in treating female athletes. I continued to attempt a comeback, which caused further injury to my knee. Later in that year, an orthopedic surgeon stated in no uncertain terms that I'd never compete again. Regardless, my brain refused to accept the diagnosis. Certain that I should be able to compete again, I continued to train. Yet, my body could no longer handle competitive sports. My dream of a successful athletic career, being a coach, and owning a training camp in the mountains of Colorado crumbled. For the next ten years I was unable to watch women's' sports: it was too painful.

In the year following the loss of my life's dream, I struggled with undiagnosed depression. At the same time, I focused on using my pain and suffering to help others. I became more actively involved in helping at risk youth through my professional work in homeless shelters and through my faith community leading Bible Studies, youth groups and music drama teams. In school, my energies were channeled into studying to become a psychologist. Meanwhile, in the late 1970s, our nation experienced significant growth in of the area of homelessness. The fact that a nation as wealthy as ours allowed its people to be homeless was difficult to swallow. Concurrently, we were destroying homes in downtown areas and not replacing them. We refused to create affordable housing, education, and health care, and livable incomes. We refused to protect and honor our people's civil rights. As a person of faith, I knew I was called to respond.

Initially, I volunteered at a church-based shelter. Later, through God's guidance and being available to Him, I was instrumental in creating a winter shelter at my church. From that winter's experience of listening to others and much prayer, we developed one of the first transitional housing programs in the country, utilizing rental units throughout the community and helping people get jobs, go to school, address other issues, and reintegrate into the community. The program worked to prevent people from becoming homeless and rapidly transitioned people out of shelters or off the streets into housing in the community. I served as Executive Director of this housing program for thirty years. It became a model for state and federal legislation, and it opened the doors for me to work as a local, state, and national consultant, and leader in the development of hundreds of local responses to homelessness and advocacy organizations, including Metropolitan Interfaith Council on Affordable Housing (MICAH), Minnesota Coalition for the Homeless, and National Coalition for the

Homeless. It was during this period (the 1980s), that I also opened a private practice as a psychologist, which I continued until 2003.

Over the last four decades, I've been appalled and angered by the greed in our society and the limited moral outcry by people of faith. How can people of faith not respond and ensure that all people in our nation have a decent, safe, and affordable place to call home? Surely we are called to use our collective resources to Bring America Home. This unresolved anger has festered over the years.

A few years after being hurt in sports and unable to compete again, I started to drink socially. For twenty-five years I drank on and off, sometimes too much, but overall I functioned well most of the time. As I moved into my 50s, however, my body began to change with the onset of menopause. My brain became more obsessed in utilizing alcohol to escape and tolerate situations. My body couldn't handle the amount of alcohol my head wanted, and I began having more and more difficulties at work, dealing with my dad's death, my health, my relationship with God and others, and then with the legal system.

Even after two outpatient treatments, I refused to accept that I had a disease called alcoholism. My brain could not believe that something that had provided me an escape from my workaholism, athleticism, caretakerism, and perfectionism would turn on me, almost destroy me, and hurt my relationship with God, my family, friends, co-workers, and life's work.

It DID.

* * *

The term "alcoholic" is a detestable one; I hate it in the same way that I hate the terms "deformed" and "the homeless." The stereotypical assumptions made by our society when hearing these terms are cruel at best. The terms are degrading and demean the uniqueness of each human being; they devalue the person, reducing them to nothing more than a throw away, in their worst usage. I shunned the term alcoholic in my first two outpatient treatment programs: it is not all of who I am. Looking back, I can see more clearly that the term "alcoholic" prevented me from moving forward and accepting that I had a disease called "alcoholism": as with my knee injury, my body would never again be able to tolerate what my mind was demanding of it.

This devotional is my wrestling with God to understand and accept the disease of alcoholism, as well as other "–isms" within, and to discover and learn what recovering is all about. I do not describe myself as an alcoholic, because I don't believe that this disease of alcoholism defines me, just as I don't define others by their disease, even though many of their life choices may have been a factor in developing their disease just as my life choices have impacted the development of my disease of alcoholism.

Writing helped me better understand myself by concretely identifying what happened in my life, and what were precursors to developing the disease of alcoholism. I began with writing in my prayer journal, and then moved on to this devotional. I wanted to confront my denial of the disease and document the impact on my relationship with God, myself, others and my life work. I also wanted to identify what I had learned as I wrestled with God about these issues and put into action the changes I would need to make and maintain to be a well-being.

I struggled with whether I would use the term "battle" or the term "wrestle" as I attempted to articulate this portion of my journey with God. I was reminded of Jacob's wrestling with God. Also, I reviewed the definitions of "wrestle" and "wrestling": To combat an opposing tendency or force. To engage in deep thought, consideration, or debate. To engage in or as if in a violent or determined struggle." "Wrestle" and "wrestling" seemed to be the words that fit the struggle I was and still have with God in my heart, soul, mind and body

As I wrestled with God over the last twenty four months, I studied in-depth Biblical scripture, the tenets of the Oxford Group (the basis for Alcoholic Anonymous), the 12 steps of AA, the original text of the Serenity Prayer by Reinhold Niebuhr (Sifton 2005, 277), and the books *Lincoln's Battles with God* (Mansfield 2012), *Jesus Calling* (Young 2004), *The Purpose Driven Life* (Warren 2003), as well as other books and devotionals influenced the development of these forty devotions. I needed to do this for me, so I could review it, remember, and grow as a human being. As I shared portions of many of these devotions with others in AA or those struggling with other "–isms", they appeared to find comfort, a better understanding of themselves, and a different way to approach their own struggles. I don't have all the answers. In fact, I have more questions than answers. Nevertheless, this wrestling has helped me. I hope that you find it to be true for you, too!

You may be a person of faith, a person of faith who has doubts or has walked away from your faith; you may doubt or never have believed in a God or Higher Power. These descriptions describe me at various points in life, too!

Abraham Lincoln was called an atheist, agnostic, and infidel as he battled with God through his grief and depression to find faith. In Stephen Mansfield's detailed account of Lincoln's struggles with matters of faith, Mansfield shares a recollection by a friend of Lincoln's. Charged with being an "infidel," Lincoln said of the charges to his friend,

> There came into my life sad events and a loss that you knew and a great deal about how hard they were for me; for you at that time were a mutual friend. Those days of trouble found me amidst a sea of questionings. They piled big upon me, experiences that brought with them great strains upon my emotional and mental life. Through all, I groped my way until I found a stronger and higher grasp of thought, one that reached beyond this life with a clearness and satisfaction I have never known before. The Scripture unfolded before me with a deeper and more logical appeal, through these new

experiences, than anything else I could find to turn to, or ever before had found in them.

I do not claim that all doubts were removed then, or since that time have been swept away. They are not. Probably it is to be my lot to go in a twilight, feeling, and reasoning my way through life, as questioning, doubting Thomas did. But in my poor maimed, withered way, I bear with me, as I go on, a seeking spirit of desire for a faith that was with him of olden time, who, in his need, as is in mine, exclaimed: 'Help thou my unbelief.' (Mansfield 2012, 68)

I continue to struggle with doubts, anger, hurt, pain and regrets. I now choose to face them, however, with God instead of drowning them in alcohol. As I do this each day, I sense new growth and strength developing in my being and a greater peace with God, myself, and others

The cover of this devotional displays a beautiful rainbow. Rainbows typically appear after a rainstorm. God created the rainbow; in this we are reminded of his everlasting commitment and unfailing love for us. The storms in my own life will continue, both the ones I've created, and the storms of daily life: death, hurt, loss, and rejection. If I'm willing to let God's light shine through them, eventually a rainbow of hope, peace, love and understanding will occur:

> And God said, "This is the sign of the covenant which I make between me and you and every living creature that is with you, for all future generations: I set my [rain] bow in the cloud, and it shall be a sign of the covenant between me and earth." (Genesis 9: 12–13)

Throughout this devotional, I conclude each devotion with a passage from the Bible, Revised Standard Version. I encourage you to put the devotion into action immediately. I truly believe awareness does not create change. Change creates change. As we change each day, we develop new and healthier patterns of living and being.

I offer this devotional to the reader well aware that I am but a single voice, striving to live in God's Will. As Gandhi said: "I have no special revelation of God's will. My firm belief is that He reveals Himself daily to every human being, but we shut our ears to the 'still small voice'. We shut our eyes to the Pillar of Fire in front of us. I realize His omnipresence" (Young India 1921, 161–62). I now take time to be still and cease striving, so that I may hear that "still small voice" of God and let Him guide me in my on-going journey.

My hope and prayer is that this devotional will help you in your journey of recovering you.

Covered in God's love

By the time I was four years old, I was aware that I was different. I was born with a deformed smaller right hand, and the right side of my chest never fully developed. It was at age four that surgery was performed to remove webbing from between two fingers on the right hand, requiring an overnight stay in the hospital. As my mom and dad left the hospital that evening, I clearly recall the sense of abandonment I felt in that strange place with its sterile white walls. I sobbed, but later in the night, when I prayed the simple prayers that our family prayed together every evening, a powerful sense of comfort and love from God surrounded me. I've continued to experience God's presence for most of my life.

Fifty-four years later, sitting alone on my bed at the Hazelden Inpatient Treatment Center, I asked myself, how did I end up here? The previous six months had been insanity with my abuse of alcohol and prescribed medications. What had I done to my family and friends, to myself? How could I have allowed myself to drink and drive again and cause another car accident? Did I learn nothing after the first accident in 2006? I now faced a potential four years in prison for hurting others. I could lose my career, my family, and myself as well.

I argued and wrestled with myself: I don't want to be here. I had agreed to a stay of twenty-eight days, but it was clear they intend to set the plan for longer. Will I stay and try to figure this out with God, or leave as quickly as I can and take my chances?

I'd tried to run away from my problems with alcohol. It hadn't worked. And why run now? So I could go to jail sooner? If I stay, will it keep me out of jail? What about my home, cat, and finances? I hadn't thought clearly in months. With the passage of time, would my brain function properly again after the seizure, the stroke, and the coma-like state I had experienced at in the last month?

Writing in a prayer journal has been the way I've sorted out my thoughts for many years, as well as the manner in which I've talked with God on a regular basis. I scribbled a question in the journal: "Do you still love me God?" Immediately, I felt His love covering, surrounding me—the same all-encompassing peace I'd experienced as a child.

I sensed God asking me, "Do you trust me to help you?" I responded belligerently: If You can't, no one can!

I'd had three years of sobriety. Then, I began struggling again after being prescribed a pain medication for a failed root canal. I relapsed within a week. After completing a relapse program, I'd had fourteen months of sobriety, but I'm repeatedly drawn back to alcohol. Impatient and wanting to move along and be done with my present situation, I asked: God, what does it mean to recover? Can I truly recover? What is Recovery?

Gently, God let me know that I needed to be still, stay at the treatment center, and He would show me.

God is our Refuge and Strength,
a very present help in trouble.
Psalm 46:1

Action: Read Psalm 46. Write down your thoughts, prayers, and insights each day.

What happened?

As I began to write to God in a prayer journal again, it wasn't unusual for me to rant and rave about the situation I was in. The following are excerpts from my journal while at Hazelden:

➤ NO, it can't be true, but I drank for twenty-five years without any problems. Alcohol has been there to help me relax, not be so introverted and shy, it was a quick get away, and helped me tolerate situations. How could alcohol turn against me, become a disease, and now I can't ever use again?

➤ I know sometimes I drank too much, got drunk, drank when I shouldn't have, had some withdrawals and did the hangover the toilet routine. I thought about alcohol too much, and in 2 relapses I was hiding my drinking, or so I thought, from others and me.

➤ Why after menopause—drinking heavier for several years when I was (not) dealing with an organization's failings and relationships breakups—did my brain and body betray me? I could usually count on my brain to get me out of just about anything. When I was connected with God, we did incredible things. I thought I could fix just about anything.

So often in the last several years I've wrestled with God about the nature of alcoholism: is it a "disease" or a "choice"?

During both of my relapses, I chose to drink. Initially, I could quit for a few days, but the length of the time I could abstain became shorter and shorter. I cared less and drank more to get away. I lied overtly (telling others I wasn't using) or covertly (hiding alcohol and drinking alone while having no contact with others).

Alcohol became my god. I was constantly planning when, where, and how I could use in order to forget and escape life's struggles.

"BE STILL," God said.

"Don't have many other choices," was my belligerent response.

"Yes, you do. You can keep running and making excuses," God answered.

"So what is Recovery?" I asked again.

Be still, and know that I am God.
Psalm 46:10

Action: Read Psalm 46 again. Find a quiet place to be alone and Be Still. Write about your struggles with alcohol and any other addiction issues.

It's the doctors' fault: prescription medications made my drinking worse!

While at Hazelden, the ranting and raving continued in my prayer journal as I attempted to rationalize away my responsibility for my situation by blaming doctors for prescribing drugs to me:

> My drinking exponentially increased after I hurt my neck and back and was prescribed Tramadol—a non-narcotic pain killer. While I didn't drink while I physically took it, it built up in my system (as do many prescribed drugs), when I ran out, my drinking increased dramatically. I have little and no recollection of about 10 weeks in the fall of 2011. As I withdrew from Tramadol (and possibly from alcohol), I had a seizure. I was hospitalized for 2 days. Doctor said I also had experienced a stroke. I thought hospitalization would stop me.

After one hospitalization, I remained sober for about ten days, until I confronted my dad's last days on the planet. My dad was and is my hero, my primary role model, confidant, and spiritual guide in life. I was the primary caregiver for my parents for ten years. I assisted them with daily living, business issues, and developing their end of life plans. I failed, however, to set up a plan for how I would deal with their deaths.

My family's dynamics are difficult for me. They became unbearable during my dad's last days. I had been released from the hospital the previous week, and suddenly I faced my dad's imminent death without my best friend—alcohol. After only five days of being with family, I sought relief in the bottle. Although I tried to control it, after my dad died, I got drunk and went back to my parent's home. My siblings took me to the hospital. Later I was placed in detox. I felt as if I had been dumped and abandoned by my family. I stopped drinking for a month after detox, went to AA meetings, took an anti-depressant, and began individual therapy.

It seemed that all was going well, until I began dwelling on the past. At the same time, my resentment towards others increased. I saw myself as a scapegoat both for problems at work and for my family's grief and anger at the loss of our dad. Tired of fighting my own demons and feeling that I had lost everything, I began to drink again. After becoming drunk at a friend's family Christmas, I tried to stop again and went through withdrawal from alcohol. For approximately thirty-six hours, I had hallucinations. As I had in the past, I'd stopped taking all my vitamins and medications, including my antidepressant.

Hospitalized once again, I was placed on an anti-anxiety medication. It was prescribed as a temporary measure, until a place opened up for me in treatment at the end of the month. I was unaware that I should not drink while on the medication. During the next three weeks, I spent a night in jail, and I was hospitalized three more times (twice in detox, and once after I caused an accident that injured others.)

Although I was resistant to the idea of being locked up as an inpatient at Hazelden Treatment Center, I agreed to go for twenty-eight days. (In the end, I stayed for ten weeks.) It was clear that I had to face whatever was happening in my body and in my life. I felt that my brain had betrayed me. I couldn't figure it out on my own. I turned to my Bible and began to read. As I read, I began to understand that my strength, that of being a high performer who always strives to be the best, was now a weakness. I wasn't taking time to be still and to cease striving, in order to hear God when He spoke to me.

> *Be still, and know that I am God.*
> **Psalm 46:10**

Action: Read Psalm 46, sit quietly alone, and write about your life at this moment in time.

Powerless over life, not alcohol

Trying to understand what had happened in my life, I talked with God about my previous times in treatments. During my first two out-patient treatments I was out of control, but I had rationalized to myself, "I'm not like the others here."

My problem wasn't alcohol, I told myself. My problem was workaholism. I simply had turned too often to alcohol for relief, for a mini-vacation. I refused to accept that I had a disease. I couldn't give up my friend and not drink again. At the same time, while denying that I had a disease, I often found myself thinking about how I would be able to drink again "normally" after I finished probation (when no one would be watching my every move).

In my mid-twenties, I took my first drink. As an athlete, I was disciplined about everything I ate or drank. Even after training for the Olympics and having my Olympic dreams shattered by a knee injury that was misdiagnosed, I didn't drink. But a few years later, I decided to drink in order to fit in and relax. I recognized immediately that alcohol gave me a high similar to the one I experienced when training and competing in sports.

Over the years my body changed, but I hadn't taken the time to understand the chemical and hormonal changes that had occurred during the past twenty-five years of drinking. Nor was I aware that alcoholism was a problem on my father's side of the family. I was aware of sensitivity to medication on my mother's side of the family. My aunt committed suicide at about age fifty-eight, after she decided to determine her own dosage of Lithium. I was under the influence of alcohol at the doctor's appointment, when I was prescribed pain medication and was not thinking clearly when I agreed to take the medication.

My doctors prescribed medications that were dangerous for me as I struggled with alcohol, although they had access to my health records indicating my struggles with alcohol. I later discovered from doctors specializing in addictions that the combination of alcohol with the medications I was taking was potentially lethal.

Why did I desire alcohol more and more when my body could tolerate it less and less? I began reading about alcoholism, and I watched the movie "Pleasure Unwoven." Although the movie struck me as somewhat corny, it did drive home for me the importance of taking seriously the changes that may have occurred in my brain. Even so, I hoped it wasn't true.

And do not be drunk with wine, for that is
debauchery; but be filled with the Spirit . . ..
Ephesians 5:18

Action: Watch the DVD "Pleasure Unwoven" (McCauley, 2009). Writing in your journal, discuss with God who is to be in control of you: God's Spirit, or you and alcoholic spirits?

Powerless over alcohol

Sitting on my bed at Hazelden, I looked back at the past six months: it was obvious even to me that I had been out of control. My alcohol use, combined with three different prescription drugs, had taken me on a roller coaster of locked up medical placements in hospitals, detox, and now inpatient treatment. I had to face whatever was happening.

As a psychologist, retired now for nine years, I had struggled as a professional with the diagnosis of alcoholism as a disease. It seemed to me that what and how much one drank was a choice.

As I seriously studied the brain research, I began to understand and accept that my brain had changed. The dopamine high I experienced when participating in sports was replaced with an alcoholic dopamine high, but, the manner in which my brain dealt with dopamine had changed. This was further complicated by the medications prescribed, which according to several doctors I have since consulted, should not have been prescribed for me. The drugs, combined with alcohol, dramatically re-set the pleasure or relief set point higher. They further indicated that the increase in alcohol use was precipitated by the prescribed medications. The seizure, stroke, and coma-like experiences were directly related to my use of those medications and alcohol.

Alcoholism was classified as a "disease" in 1956 by the American Medical Association. It met the medical criteria that an organ (the brain) changed and that the body experienced withdrawal when the substance was not available. This last decade (2002–2012) of brain research provides a number of significant insights into the changes that take place in the brain as an individual develops an addiction. Minimal research, in my opinion, has been done on the impact of menopause and the hormonal changes that occur with women, or on the increase in alcohol use and development of alcoholism in women in their late 40s and 50s.

Intellectually, I understood all of this new information. Nevertheless, I resisted accepting the fact that I had developed the disease called "alcoholism."

> *Trust in the Lord with all your heart,*
> *and do not rely on your own insight.*
> **Proverbs 3:5**

Action: Journal for ten minutes: list other diseases such as heart disease, cancer, and diabetes, and the consequences that result when their existence is denied. Will you continue to deny the disease you have?

Dis-ease

One morning as I continued to wrestle with the acceptance that I had a disease called "alcoholism," I began to think about the word "disease." Could it be not only a medical disease, but a "dis-ease" within as well?

By and large, I drank in order to feel good, to get away, to deal with shyness, and make it easier to tolerate certain situations. There was dis-ease in my life, and I was using alcohol as a quick fix. This was similar to my use of sports during the first twenty-five years of my life to escape and feel good with an athletically induced dopamine high.

How could this simple fix of alcohol replace a God I had loved, worshiped, prayed to, and served for most of my life?

Portions of the language from AA, which I had resisted embracing, began to make sense, such as the phrase "Alcohol is cunning and baffling." It helped me understand how dangerous alcohol was for me when I was and am experiencing dis-ease (when distressed, discontented, angry, over tired, hungry, and hurt), and, how my brain will want a quick fix—alcohol.

Generally life had been going well since the relapse in 2009. Life was busy in early 2011. In my professional life, once again I took a lead role in securing statewide funding for people experiencing homelessness in the state legislature. During late spring and early summer, I overstretched myself, organizations that I led, and my finances. Additionally, I tried to do and be more than what I was capable of as I assisted my parents with their daily needs and continued with volunteer work around the country. Further, at a time when I needed a strong spiritual base, the church I attended was in turmoil, and, I believed, preached intolerance of others. I stopped attending, and as a result, isolated myself even more. I didn't seek out other spiritual support.

That summer while in Washington D.C., I received a call relaying negative comments made about my professional work. Upset, I immediately sought out alcohol for relief from my dis-ease, instead of walking and talking with God as was my habit each evening. I picked up and drank a four-pack of small bottles of chardonnay. My dis-ease lead me into a six-month downward spiral, in which I almost destroyed myself, my relationships (with God and with others), and most of what I had worked for in life.

As I wrestled with the idea of "dis-ease," I thought, that's a pretty good summary of what had happened. I then wrote it down and identified the signs that were red flags signaling that I was in trouble: thinking about the purchase of alcohol, craving the escape and sense of relief it provided, and spending more time with people who drank. I also made a list of the names of the people I could call when I was struggling. I put it in my wallet.

Have no anxiety about anything, but in everything by prayer and supplication with thanksgiving, let your requests be made known to God. And the peace of God, which passes all understanding, will keep your hearts and your minds in Christ Jesus.
Philippians 4:6–7

Action: Be still and know God when dis-ease enters your life. Write down your warning signals as well as the names and numbers of people you can call when you are struggling, and put it in your wallet.

Surrendering

As I began treatment again, I was told that as yet, I didn't understand or fully comprehend Step One of Alcoholics Anonymous: I needed to admit not only that I was out of control with my workaholism, but also that I had a disease called alcoholism, and a dis-ease with life.

In addition to reading materials related to Alcoholics Anonymous, I read Narcotics Anonymous. In reading of Step One of Narcotics Anonymous, I gained a clearer understanding of what I had missed during the first two outpatient treatments, for it focused on integrity, and integrity is a characteristic I highly value. As a psychologist, I taught the folks that I served, no one is perfect; however, whether a person has integrity and can be trusted, most often can be determined if what they say they will do matches up at least ninety percent of the time with what they actually do.

When in a frenzy of working, experiencing dis-ease, or when drinking, I was dishonest, or, to be blunt, I lied in order to do what I wanted to do. In truth, **I didn't care about what I'd said I'd do**.

I had little or no integrity when I drank, and I was powerless to maintain my integrity, to be the me I wanted to be. Alcohol consumed my thoughts: when, where, and how I could get another drink and receive some relief from my body's withdrawal. This obsession with alcohol had become the focus of my life instead of God.

Was I willing to admit and accept what I knew was true? Would I surrender not only my workaholism and dis-ease, but also my disease of alcoholism to God? Was I willing to say, as in one of my mother's favorite hymns, "I surrender all" to God? It's a question I have to answer every day, many times throughout the day. Will I believe, have faith, surrender and put myself in God's hand?

Yes, I said. It's clear that I need to live differently.

"Good! I'll teach you even more," God said gently.

Behold, I have graven you on the palms of my hand . . ..
Isaiah 49:16a

Action: Draw a picture of yourself in the palm of God's Hand.
Journal about how you feel being in God's hand.

Re-Covering

What was I missing? What did I not understand? I'd been spending time with God before this relapse—praying, journaling and reading most mornings. Yet, I chose to drink and allow myself to be caught up in the disease of alcoholism again.

In truth, I wasn't surrendering each moment to God. I wasn't running for cover in God when the desires attacked me to drink and escape my problems, relax, or forget about the struggles of life. I thought I could handle it myself. I was dead wrong, almost literally. God's protective care of those in the car I hit and of me, allowed me another chance to live.

God has always had a hold of my hand, even as I tried to strain and go where I shouldn't, much like my mom and dad would hold my hand as I crossed the street as a child. They reminded me to look both ways, make sure there were no cars or danger, and then cross. They held my hand to pull me back in case I didn't follow directions or raced out into traffic.

God had pulled me back from danger many times in life. Mostly, I had listened. It was different now—alcohol was more powerful than it had been before. As a disease, my mind was obsessed with the desire for more and more. It controlled my body. I needed it more and more to feel "normal," yet my body couldn't handle it any more.

I sensed God saying," Sue, take your small deformed right hand and put it into your larger left hand. I will never let go of your hand. But you also need to run to Me like you did as a child running to your bed and covering up in your blankets, away from thunder, arguments, and all your troubles. Let Me cover you in My Hand with My Spirit protecting you from those other spirits of alcoholism, workaholism, and, yes, perfectionism. Not once, but as often as you choose, come and be re-covered in Me each day. Then those other spirits can't have control of you because you are in Me, and I am in you."

"So that's what You mean by "re-covering." It's me being re-covered in Your Spirit each day and each moment, if I think I need to or not," I said proudly, thinking I got it now.

I sensed God smiling patiently and saying, "Yes," then gently, "You will always need Me."

For I, the Lord Your God,
hold your right hand;
it is I who say to you, "Fear not,
I will help you."
Isaiah 41:13

Action: Look at the picture you drew of yourself in God's Hand. Imagine God's fingers gently covering, comforting and protecting you. Write about how it feels to know that God is with you, comforting and protecting you.

Human "doer," or human "being"?

Most of my life has been spent in helping others, because I believed God called me to do so, to share what I had, for I certainly had more resources than many on the planet. I learned this early in life. My parents and church had taught me it is better to give than to receive.

In addition, my mother suffered from migraines. Many times I took care of her and the household chores. I recognized early that taking care of others and working hard resulted in appreciation and praise.

This "helping" eventually became taking care of others at the expense of my own needs. It created difficult situations when it led to overdoing, over committing, and utilizing more resources than I had to give. I didn't understand God's command to love Him and love others as myself. I didn't understand what it meant to be a human being. Instead, I came to believe that I loved Him, I loved others, but I didn't need much from others.

While in treatment, I again thought about the difference between being a human "doer" and a human "being." As a workaholic, I became a human doer. I lost any sense that I was anything other than what I did. Indeed, workaholism often precipitated my return to alcohol as I sought relief from the stress and obligations I had put on myself. Was my work me? Or was my work an expression of who I am? More often than I care to admit, my work was me.

In Exodus 3:14, God describes himself as "I Am Who I Am"; as being—"I Am," not as "I Am What I Am Doing." So, if I am to be re-covered in God, how will I define myself? I know I am His child, but who am I as a human "being"? As I played with the word "being," I talked with God and began to see it in a new way:

Being

Be in G(od). Be in God.   I'm a human being. I am to… ___Be in G___od.

Now, the Biblical injunction "Be still and know I am God" made more sense. This verse can be translated also as "to cease striving [or for me, stop working] and know that I am God." I need to stop everything and know and be in, abide, in God.

Being re-covered in God is not only for the times I need God to protect me, rather, it is so that at **all times** I can be fully human and alive in God. To paraphrase John Powell, it is to "transcend my purely self-directed concern and discover meaning in my life by utilizing and sharing the gifts and passions God has given me to love others and let them love me" (Powell 1976, 26–27).

[Jesus said:] Abide in Me, and I in you.
John 15:4a

Action: Write "Be in God" ten times. Then write (your name) in God ten times. Journal about how life would be different if you lived each day "being" in God?

Seeing life honestly: knowing the truth, and letting truth set me free

I've always thought of myself as an honest person: that is, what I say and do matches up most of the time.

I respect integrity. My dad was a man of great integrity, and I want to be a solid person of God like him. He was, however, a workaholic, and he tended to be perfectionist. Even so, he always took the time to be present at his children's athletic, musical, and school events. He appeared to be able to do it all very well. He drank little alcohol. It was seldom in our home except later in my adult life at holidays or parties.

Over time it became clear that he was fearful of alcohol, although his family didn't talk about it, or admit there were any issues. I didn't understand these fears, until after I caused my first accident when drinking and driving, and he explained how he had hoped the alcoholism on his side of the family had skipped my generation, and that his children had escaped the disease.

Being honest about feelings or about situations was discouraged at times in my family. It appeared to me that looking good, acting properly, saying the right thing, and being successful were valued above saying what was true and what was happening in reality. As a consequence, expressing and discussing feelings was not something I did with others. I had tried a few times and been hurt, so I chose to keep my feelings to myself. I talked bluntly with God in my prayer journals, and I often had discussions with myself. This was not enough: the intensity of my feelings would emerge oddly at times—I'd cry or become upset about matters unrelated to the present moment when I was hurt physically, mad at myself, or when watching a performance, movie, or sentimental commercial.

28

So, even though I was a retired psychologist who had encouraged others to talk about their feelings, I didn't. Instead of being honest about how events impacted me and how I felt, I used work, exercise, caretaking, and alcohol to avoid discussing difficult issues, and I denied many of my feelings.

Looking back on my life, I recognize that I became more and more dishonest with others and myself as alcohol gained importance and played a greater role in my life. Then, as it became a disease, it nearly destroyed my life. I lied about whether I was drinking or not. I lied about what I was doing, where I had been, what types of relationships I was having, and about my relationship with myself and with God.

I had to choose: would I once again deny that I have a disease called "alcoholism" and simply do what was required to get out of treatment, or would I face myself, face God, and then others?

It was clear that I couldn't be free to have a real relationship with God, myself, or others unless I was honest and truthful about myself and alcohol.

God is Spirit, and those who worship him
must worship in spirit and truth.
John 4:24

Action: Make a list of those situations and times you have been dishonest and lied during the last year.

Self

I couldn't address the truth about my lies until I faced that I wanted to be more than I am. I needed to understand, again, that which is so visibly clear to me in creation: I am NOT the Creator of the heavens and earth. I do not control events, situations, things or people. I am one person alive only through the breath and will of God the Creator, here for a twinkling of an eye in history.

My self-sacrificing, self-justification, self-seeking, self-sufficiency and other self-defeating behaviors are a big part of the lie I tell myself. It was much easier for me to maintain those lies as I drank. Initially, drinking simply helped me relax enough to socialize and escape from the daily pressures. As the daily pressures increased I drank more and more, rather than deal with the root causes of my dis-ease. Just like a dam breaks when under too much pressure from flood waters, my body was breaking down. It couldn't handle the amount of alcohol my brain wanted to get relief from the pressures in life.

With alcohol as my god, I was lost in the valley of the shadow of death. I ran to alcohol for refuge, and the alcohol spirits took over—my brain was obsessed by it, and my body couldn't tolerate it.

When I'm sober, I do have control over my choice of whether I will accept the free will God has given me to choose Him, or if I will turn to other spirits. I exist only because the Great I Am Who I Am gives me life. My talents and abilities are God given, too. I can only be if I am in God. I can only be in God if I am in truth about who I am—a beloved creation of the Almighty God. When I have known and lived this in life, God has used His Power to do incredible things through me as I was available to Him.

To live in truth, honesty, and freedom, I must daily (sometimes moment by moment) choose to be in God.

This means facing honestly my lies, faults, and failings. But will God still love me and want me? I imagine seeing God smirk every time I say this. God being God knows all my lies, but He wants me to admit them, so that I'll face them with Him, myself, and others.

> *[For Jesus said,] I will never forsake or abandon you.*
> **Hebrews 13:5b**

Action: Utilizing prefix self, identify the terms that describe you trying to be God.

Telling the truth to God

One of my favorite Psalms is Psalm 139. It describes the uniqueness in how God created each of us, how special we are to Him, and how He is with us always.

This is my paraphrase of the first few verses: O Lord, thou has searched me and know me You know when I sit down and rise up, You know my thoughts from afar. You are acquainted with all my ways and even before a word is on my tongue You know it.

It was time for me to face God in all honesty. I talked with Him truthfully about my attempts to play god and be more than I am. I talk about my self-sacrificing behaviors—helping and taking care of others who had no homes, families, others that cared for them often at the expense of my own health, family, and financial stability, my self-seeking—whenever I was insecure, I wanted attention and the recognition for all the good work I had done. I talked with Him of my self-righteous behavior—speaking negatively about people with resources because they weren't sharing as much as I thought they should. I talked of my self- justification—making excuses for not getting things done that I had promised to do; of the way I put myself down for not doing what I perceived to be enough, and trying to do everything perfectly, in spite of the fact that nothing I can or ever will do will be absolutely perfect.

I was honest with God about my lies. I'd lied about drinking again. I'd lied about how much I could handle. I'd lied about my feelings of anger, hurt, and resentments in life. I'd lied about trusting Him to take care of me and ran to alcohol for relief instead. I'd lied about relationships, how lonely I was at times, how hurt I was by people yelling or putting me down. I'd lied about my fears. I'd lied about liking to drink only to relax and be social, when in truth, it was often to tolerate difficult situations and escape my own pain.

I cried out in anguish to God. I've lied about so many things—I was wrong, I'm sorry, please forgive me, and help me correct and direct my paths by being in You.

Search me, O God, and know my heart!
Try me and know my thoughts!
And see if there be any wicked way in me,
and lead me in the way everlasting!
Psalm 139:23–24

Action: Read Psalm 139. Write to God and identify what you have lied about in life.

Telling the truth to another person

During outpatient treatment, Alcoholics Anonymous meetings, and inpatient treatment, I was told again and again by those who were staying sober, "Find a sponsor." I didn't want a sponsor. I told myself, I can do this on my own. I didn't want anyone telling me what to do. Anyway, they wouldn't understand the work I do, or the issues I'm dealing with.

My self-righteousness surfaced in full force to keep me from reaching out and asking for help. I wrestled with God for a solution.

The word sponsor had a connotation **that just didn't fit for me**. As I talked with God, other words came to mind: teacher, disciple, coach, and mentor. These are concepts I'd known and utilized in learning more about God, social justice, and as an athlete.

My first extended experience of telling the truth about myself to another person took place during the five-week intensive outpatient program at Hazelden. I met with one of the spiritual directors for a couple hours and shared with her what I resented in life, and the truth about my fears and relationships. It was a cleansing experience to tell my experience to another, admit what I had done wrong, accept responsibility for creating harmful situations, and how all of this impacted my life.

In preparing for our meeting, I wrote down all my resentments, fears, and sexual issues in relationships. I was amazed as I looked at the truth of my life and realized that I had struggled with many of these issues for years, and that I used alcohol to make myself numb in order to avoid facing and taking responsibility for the truth about myself.

I knew that before I left Hazelden, I would need to experiment with this idea of someone on the "outside" that I would connect with on a regular basis. The idea of a temporary sponsor sounded good. I could check them out, and they could check me out to see if we fit. I also knew that my friends who didn't have the disease were unable to understand the changes that had happened to me. While they wanted to be supportive, they couldn't get it in the same way as someone who has the disease can.

Although my first two temporary "sponsors" were unable to provide consistent support, I surprised myself: I didn't give up on the idea. I prayed that God would guide me to someone who believed in Him and could help me continue my journey without alcohol.

Further, I was blessed greatly by the renewal of my acquaintance with a woman that I'd met when I attended AA after my first DUI (Driving Under the Influence) accident. She, unlike me, had taken the advice of others and had a strong support person and maintained sobriety for almost eight years. She has guided me, prayed with me, and mentored me, as I've told her my truths, struggles, and shared my own insights as I continue to re-cover each day in God.

For where two or three are gathered in my
name, there am I in the midst of them.
Matthew 18:20

Action: Find someone who you can tell the truth to, and ask that person to support you. Call him or her every day for ten days.

Resentments

When I stopped drinking, my feelings of anger towards myself, others, and situations often seemed more than I could handle. When I drank, I didn't face or deal with feelings: I simply numbed them. But the feelings came back even stronger, so I drank more. It was a vicious cycle that sometimes sent me spiraling out of control.

It brings to mind an illustration I've shared with others for decades: When I'm in the house and flies have gotten in, I brush them away. But they keep coming back buzzing around my head or landing on me. I can either continue to brush them away and have some temporary relief, or, I can get a fly swatter, kill them one at a time, and then sit down to enjoy the peaceful quietness without being bugged.

To find peace within, I needed to learn how to deal with my feelings, especially anger, which often surfaced later as resentment. The resentments were my perceptions that people were not doing their share in various situations, not meeting my needs, or that what they said (especially people of faith) and what they did didn't match up.

I read the book *Drop the Rock: Removing Character Defects* (2005, Hazelden Foundation). The title itself was helpful as I thought about resentments. Typically my anger starts with one situation, and like a rock in my shoe, it becomes increasingly irritating when I walk. I have a choice: get the rock out of my shoe, or have a painful walk, and perhaps develop a sore on my foot. On the other hand, if I take the rock out of my shoe and drop it on the ground, the walk is more enjoyable. If I take the rock and put it in my pocket and continue thinking about it, I may eventually have a pocket full of rocks to lug around.

I tried an experiment while walking the trails at Hazelden. When I thought of something I resented, I picked up a rock and put it in my pocket. It didn't take long before my pockets were full. My walk became unpleasant. If I wanted to enjoy my walk, I needed to take each rock out of my pocket, and drop it. My walk became easier, more pleasant and more enjoyable.

I must remind myself of this illustration when I feel angry. I need to feel my anger, accept it as a feeling (no one made me angry, it was my response), and decide to deal with it and drop it; otherwise, I run the risk of my anger becoming resentment and turning my walk in life into a painful and miserable one.

As I've learned to feel again, I continually remind myself that feelings are helpful gut responses to a situation. Feelings can provide incredible information for making intelligent decisions. Feelings, however, are horrible decision makers on their own. If I don't address them immediately, those little feelings, like little pebbles, continue to irritate me, and I blow them up into bigger issues than they are. The resentments become like larger and larger rocks weighing me down, and I make my life miserable. Drop the Rock(s)!

Be angry, but do not sin; do not let the sun
go down on your anger . . . .
Ephesians 4:26

Action: Read the book *Drop the Rock*. Take a walk and pick up a rock for each of your resentments. Carry it on your walk for ten minutes, and then drop one rock at a time. Journal about your experience.

Fears

I grew up in a family with high expectations: look good, be successful, be smart, be the best, and be a good, God-loving person. This was in the 1950s and 1960s when our American society was involved in significant changes: the Civil Rights movement; Vietnam War protests; women's athletic rights; an explosion of scientific knowledge, information, and computers; a "Me" generation ("doing your own thing"); a society questioning if God was dead or alive; and rapidly changing and competitive national and international economic markets.

All of these factors influenced my personal and professional development. As I met certain expectations, I received a great deal of praise, encouragement and support. I continued to accept my childhood interpretation of praise to mean that not only must I be good, but I must also be the best (or perfect) in order to earn praise, respect, and love from others.

My genuine God-given, deep concern and caring for others often turned into a self-made trap. I would entangle myself in caretaking roles with others. Somehow my mind had decided that, if I took care of others well, they would need me, want me, and thus, love me.

Being loved and accepted had become twisted from being a free gift one person gives another to a transaction based upon how well I performed. My workaholism, perfectionism, and caretakerism provided the means to get what I wanted. But they also created incredible fears: What if I failed? What if I couldn't get it all done? What if I didn't know everything and didn't do it perfectly? What if I couldn't be there when someone needed me? I was plagued with doubts and fears and ruminated upon them day after day.

Imagine blowing up several balloons. You don't want anyone to see them, but you have no string with which to tie them down. You try to cover them up with your body, but it doesn't work. Your energy becomes focused on keeping people from seeing your balloons.

Imagine that the doubts and fears about not being perfect, not getting everything done perfectly, not knowing everything, or not being there when someone needs me is the air I blow into my balloons. I don't want anyone to see my balloons filled with imperfections and fears, so I spend a great deal of time and energy attempting to cover them up. How can I enjoy life if my days are consumed with keeping these balloons hidden? Alcohol provides an escape, but it's a temporary and dangerous fix.

Eventually I learned that it was my hot air that had blown up those fears and balloons. I had to admit and face my fears; then, I could let the air out. Amazingly, the balloons filled with my fears weren't such a big deal after all. Naturally, there are times when I let the hot air out, and it squeals much like the balloon does if you pull on its mouthpiece when letting the air out. Nonetheless, it's my own squealing from exhaustion after trying to be more than I am or can be.

To be me, I had to change my fear-based pleasing-others behavior to that of a genuine, gentle, humble, person, discovering and expanding my love of God, myself, and others. Life, thus, has become more and more each day, a great adventure of loving and enjoying life instead of fearing it or running away from it.

There is no fear in love, but perfect love casts out fear.
I John 4:18a

Action: Blow up five balloons. Walk around for a few minutes trying to hide them from view. Imagine that the air you blew into your balloons are your fears. List the fears, as well as what thoughts you maintain that keep those fears afloat. What would life be like if you were not afraid?

Sexual Issues

I was sexually abused as a child. Like many others, I minimized the experience by telling myself that millions of others have experienced sexual abuse and rape, and I simply needed to move on. The fact is, the abuse did impact many aspects of my life including my trust of others, my personal boundaries, my sexual thoughts, as well as my comfort with intimate and sexual relationships.

Although I've discussed my abuse with clergy, close friends, and in therapy, I didn't understand how alcohol was impacting my ability to address realistically its impact on my life.

I began looking seriously at the impact of the abuse when I was sober for three years after my first treatment. I decided to be celibate at that time as I sorted through my life and the choices I made. I realized then that most of my intimate and sexual relationships were when I had been drinking alcohol. The recognition alarmed me. My marriage ended in divorce, and several relationships ended very abruptly, partially due to their or my relationship with alcohol.

My choice to be celibate and sober has impacted my relationships with others. While some close relationships have continued and developed in other ways, typically with a greater respect for each other's uniqueness and greater depth of dialogue and sharing of our spirituality, other relationships have faded away.

Using alcohol helped me to relax and feel more comfortable in intimate sexual relationships. It also made me energized and more sexually stimulated, which I understand from others with and without the disease of alcoholism is a common occurrence (but especially with those of us with the disease). It helped me to put aside my dis-ease with being close to another person. The early stages of the disease allowed me to drink at higher levels than most others without the impact. At times, I lived a life of dishonesty, dissipation, debauchery, partying, being close to folks I shouldn't have been, and hurtful to others.

While I choose to be celibate today, it's a choice each person needs to make. I know that alcohol in my system clouded my judgment in the past, and I made many unhealthy choices, especially around relationships. I know that my re-covering in God must be my primary relationship, and I must take care of myself. As I love myself as God loves me, I am able to love others. My love for myself has to be genuine and honest, with God and myself. As I grow more and more in this area, my comfort with and genuine love deepens for others.

> *Look carefully then how you walk, not as unwise men but*
> *as wise, making the most of your time, because the days*
> *are evil. Therefore do not be foolish, but understand what*
> *the will of the Lord is. And do not get drunk with wine, for*
> *that is debauchery; but be filled with the Spirit . . ..*
> **Ephesians 5:15–18**

Action: Write about your intimate and sexual relationships that were alcohol related. If you had not been drinking, would those relationships have been different? How do you want to be with others?

My plans (control), or Communion with God

Control is a huge issue for many of us. I recall one morning in particular where it came into play. I had promised to pickup and drive a gal home. She was being released from prison. We had met when I spent twelve days in jail, after I was sentenced for my second DUI accident. I was excited to help her get home so she could be with her baby who had just turned two.

I hurried to locate a map on-line. My computer repeatedly crashed or attempted to update itself and wouldn't let me download the map. I wanted the map NOW! My serenity from earlier in the morning dissipated. I called my dear friend, as I do each morning, and vented my frustration. She, too, was having a frustrating day, but her words at end the call, while simple, were profound: "You probably should just get going." I sensed God saying the same thing, and that He would guide me there. I gathered my things, dumped the computer in my backpack, and headed out the door. This experience reinforced what I have done throughout life. I tend to reach out to God in one of three ways: when I talk to Him about my plans for the day, when I'm in trouble, or in need of help with a major decision. I often neglect to ask Him for something as simple as directions.

Earlier that morning, I had read Sarah Young's *Jesus Calling*, a daily devotional written as if Jesus is talking to the reader: "Walk with Me in Holy Trust, responding to My initiatives rather than trying to make things fit in your plans … that includes compulsive planning" (Young 2004, 117). I thought, God wants me to let Him determine the day's plan, not for my plan to be in charge of the day. God knows how intense, full, restless, and at times irrational, my thinking can be. I have often wondered why He risked giving us a free will to choose between what pleases us, or to be in His Will.

Even after years of being in His Will, at any moment I can let my thoughts mess me up and go against His Will. He wants me to talk with Him about everything, even my feelings throughout the day. This may mean I don't get everything done on my list for the day. As He reminds me, it's not my responsibility to control or fix everything or everyone. It's my choice each moment of every day to be in God's Will, communing in His Spirit, living and knowing His Peace.

While I believe that I have heard God say many of these words to me before, I didn't really hear, listen and integrate those messages into how I lived each moment. For me to be re-covered in God, I not only needed to surrender intellectually that I'm not in control and let Him keep the alcoholic and other spirits from controlling me, but I need to choose to be in common union (communion) with His Spirit guiding and directing me. I must choose to be available to and for His Spirit to love and create through me.

This is easier for me to say than to actually live out: being versus doing. Listening to "just get going," I made it through rush hour traffic, asked for directions when I got close, and I was at the prison early. I ended up waiting an hour, and instead of being upset thinking I was wasting time, I apologized to God for trying to control the day. I then wrote some encouraging notes to others. When I finished the notes, the gal I had come to pick up was released and God shared His love with her as we travelled to her parent's home.

. . . [T]o set the mind on the Spirit is Life and Peace.
Romans 8:6b

Action: Write what your plans are for today. Give it up to God, and be in communion with His Spirit to guide and direct you, knowing that it may not be His plan for you today, and you may not complete everything on **your list.**

Communion, cooperation, and community

An awesome union with the Creator occurs as His Spirit dwells within me, and I feel fully alive and at peace. And so, I believe, as we are told in Matthew 22:38, "Loving the Lord your God with all your heart, soul and mind" is the way to this communion of one Spirit.

Enjoy every moment you can when you experience this communion with God. It provides me a peace that passes all understanding and renews my strength and desire to be all God wants me to be. God also asks me to cooperate with how He has created life. Intellectually this makes sense to me since He is the Creator. He wants me to have a good life, and He wants me to live life in a good orderly direction.

When I bought my Jeep it came with an owner's manual. Some of it I understood, and some of it I didn't. I know that I must put gas in the gas tank, check the oil, have the oil changed on a regular basis, and take it in to an expert on Jeeps for repairs: they have the knowledge and experience. I can decide at any point not to put gas in my Jeep, and it will eventually come to a stop. Or, I can choose not to check the oil or get it changed and my engine will likely seize up. I can also decide I know everything and attempt to fix my Jeep by taking it apart, only to find myself surrounded by its parts unable to put it back together.

In life I can cooperate with God on how He has designed life, or I can try to make it up as I go. If I choose the latter, the results will be similar to that of my Jeep when I don't attend to it properly.

So how do I learn to cooperate and learn to live with God? First and foremost is to develop a life of communing with God each day, and throughout each day. Second, read and study His writings and writings that others have written that are consistent with God's word. Third, live in community with others who love God will all their heart, soul, mind, and strength, and develop a common unity with others by sharing, caring and helping each other. I find this in churches, Alcoholics Anonymous (AA), Narcotics Anonymous (NA), Bible study, or anywhere I can share my life story and struggles and others do the same, without being judged or someone trying to fix the other. Additionally, it will include finding experts who have knowledge and experience in dealing with major issues—this may be a mentor, coach, sponsor, or pastor— someone to go to on a regular basis for help with life's general maintenance and tune-ups before a breakdown occurs.

As I move on in this journey becoming a well being, it will be dependent upon my choice to be in communion with God, cooperate with how He created life, live in community with others, and have a knowledgeable and experienced person(s) that I choose to help me learn to be well.

> . . . *[L]et us consider how to stir up one another to love and good works, not neglecting to meet together. . ..*
> **Hebrews 10:24–25a**

Action: Participate in an AA, NA, Bible Study, or other support group and journal about the experience.

Loving others as myself

As I learn to be in communion with God and cooperate with how He created life, He also tells me to love others as myself. For me to cooperate with Him, I need to be sober so I can understand how He views me and love myself as He loves me. *So God created man in His own image, in the image of God he created him; male and female he created them. . . . And God saw everything that he had made, and behold, it was **very good*** (Gen. 1:27, 31a, emphasis mine). God sees me as very good. He knew me and what I would look like before I was born. He thinks I'm wonderful and created me uniquely at this point in time in history. He has given me specific gifts and talents to be used for the common good.

In Psalm 139, the psalmist speaks of how God was there as we were created in our mother's womb, the days were formed for us. Wonderful are Thy works!

Now there are varieties of gifts; but the same Spirit, and there are a variety of service, but the same Lord; and there are varieties of working, but it is the same God who inspires them all in everyone. To each is given the manifestation of the Spirit for the common good (I Corinthians 12:4-5). Each person has been created uniquely by God's Spirit with special gifts, talents, and passions to share with others.

We are God's workmanship, created to do good works (Eph. 2:10). Another translation uses the word "poem" instead of "workmanship." I am God's handcrafted work of art, a unique creation on this planet at this time in history to be for the common good.

So what are these gifts, talents, and assets that God has given me, and how do I know? God has given each of us passions in life, things that give us energy, make our heart jump for joy, and that we learn naturally and do well.

Through my life experiences and what I've been told by people who love me, I believe that God made me smart, analytical, prophetic, organized, caring, compassionate, inclusive, helpful, disciplined, simple, loving, good at encouraging others, and a good listener.

I am a child of God. God sees me as a *very good* creation, formed the way He wanted me (deformities included), and I am a work of art in progress, a unique creation with special talents and abilities to be used for the common good. This is God's view of me and every human being. For me to move forward in life, each day I will need to make the choice to live life my own way, or choose to agree with His view of life, integrate His view, and through daily communion with Him, live life in His Will. Today, I choose His Will.

. . . [F]or in him all things were created, in heaven and on earth, visible and invisible . . . all things were created in him and for him.
Colossians 1:16

Action: Write how life would be if you saw yourself as God sees you? List your talents, gifts, and assets.

Assets and Liabilities

If I choose to live my life in Communion with God and utilize the gifts and talents he has given me, I'm an asset to the common good.

If I chose to live without God, those gifts and talents are motivated by me, not God's Will, and they become liabilities (or deficits as we say in AA) to the common good. Put bluntly, instead of being an asset, I become an ass.

Those wonderful talents and abilities that God has blessed me with change into deficits and liabilities when I choose to live in my self's will. Here are some examples of how I experience assets and liabilities in my life:

> When I'm in God's Will, He can utilize the analytical, intelligent mind He has given me to sort out answers to complex issues. When I use my own will and use my analytical, intelligent mind, I act like a know-it-all and become critical of everyone else's ideas and solutions.
> God has given me a genuine caring, helpful, and encouraging love for others, which can be incredibly helpful to others when I'm in His Will. These same gifts become liabilities when I think it's my job to please others, take care of them, or fix the world, and often I do it at my own expense, failing to take care of myself.
> God made me a very compassionate person through lessons I've learned struggling through many issues including my physical deformities. Being with another person with their suffering can be a powerful healing process in God's Spirit. It becomes a liability when I cross the boundary from being with others to thinking I can heal them.

In treatment, I made a list of my assets, liabilities and some of the warning signs I could identify when I was moving from being an asset to God, others, and myself to being a liability. This has helped me to focus on maintaining the *very good* God has created me to be and to utilize His gifts as an asset for the common good on our planet.

But I say, walk by the Spirit, and do not gratify the desires of the flesh. For the desires of the flesh are against the Spirit, and the desires of the Spirit are against the flesh; for they are opposed to each other, to prevent you from doing what you would.
Galatians 5:16–17

Action: Make a list of your assets and liabilities. How do you want to live life? Will you choose God's Spirit or your Self be in control of your life?

Walking in the light of forgiveness

A favorite part of my day is early morning as the earth rotates towards the sun. The sun rises in our eastern sky, and a slight light appears on the horizon, followed by a burst of beautiful reds, yellows, and purples. Then morning breaks, and the sun becomes a yellow ball of light that grows larger and brighter each moment. Robins, cardinals, and chickadees sing sweet songs; squirrels and rabbits run and hop; and occasionally, a deer or red fox is sighted in our suburban neighborhood.

My day begins with a walk in this early morning light. Often, I watch my shadow while walking. When I walk towards the sun, my shadow is behind me. When I walk away from the sun, my shadow is in front of me and becomes my primary focus.

When I live as God intends employing the assets he has given me, I face and live in His light. When I live in my own desires, including allowing spirits such as alcohol control me, I hide in the shadows.

But what of my past when I've lived in the shadows? What of my self-willed behaviors? God will forgive them, if I ask for forgiveness, and if I'm willing to change directions and walk in His light.

It sounds too easy. What about all my mistakes, my sins, what I haven't done out of faith or in His Will? God, do they simply go away? God gently lets me know that he has forgiven me; he no longer sees them when he looks at me. My mistakes and sins remain part of my personal history, but they are forgiven.

Life is a beautiful, unfulfilled tapestry, and I must choose who will be in control of weaving it. When I play god and weave it myself, threads of the tapestry break, tear and tangle marring its beauty. When I choose God's Will and weave it utilizing all the assets He created in me, the interlacing of threads creates a beautiful, creative, and masterful tapestry.

No tapestry is perfect, nor am I. The natural consequences of my past must be lived with, yet it doesn't have to define who I am, or where I'm going. First, however, I must be willing to ask for forgiveness from God, make a change, and turn toward His light. It's a choice I must make each moment of each day, if God is to create in me new life.

This is the covenant that I will make with the house of Israel after those days, says the Lord: I will put my laws into their minds, and write them on their hearts.. . . For I will be merciful toward their iniquities, and I will remember their sins no more.
Hebrews 8:10a, 12b

Action: Take a walk. Watch your shadow change as you turn toward and away from the sun.

You might also visit a museum, or browse in a book or on-line at the elegance, detailed, unique creativity of tapestries.

Forgiving myself

Knowing that God forgives me, gives me hope: a light at the end of the tunnel. Yet, I, myself, am my greatest obstacle. Am I willing to identify, admit, and claim my own deficits and faults? Am I willing to own the thoughts and actions that I use to justify my self-worth and behavior?

So why do I need to justify or make excuses when I'm wrong, when I've made a mistake, or when I'm late? I do so, because I'm playing god and expect myself to be perfect and in control. This is not a new insight I've reached this conclusion a number of times (typically, after a major crisis). Yet it seems to be a lesson not learned, one lost in the memory banks, or is it that I simply choose to ignore any warning signals?

The constant conversation in my head of pre-planning what will happen, arguing with someone not there about how they misunderstood or treated me poorly, or justifying my every move steals the present by focusing on things that can't be changed from the past and planning a future that may never occur. All of this keeps me so busy that I never have to see myself in God's Light of truth. I repeatedly stumble over myself and my own issues, including my denial of having the disease of alcoholism.

It's like walking into a dark room where I've left many things on the floor, rather than putting them away properly at the time. I stumble across the room trying to reach the other side. I could, instead, flip the switch that turns on the power for the light, in order to see what I need to clean up, avoid or walk around.

I can choose daily to accept and use God's power and moment by moment turn on the light of truth so that I may discern what my issues are, and which situations and people I need to avoid.

It may, at times, feel like the light comes on automatically as happens when a room has a motion sensor. Most often, however, given my ingrained patterns, I must make a conscious decision to allow God's power in my life to provide light. Each of us is wired differently, yet the key to a light turning on is the decision to flip the switch. For me to forgive myself, I need to be willing to see myself in God's Light.

I can't truly love and forgive others until I can do it daily with myself. God's truth and forgiveness can only be experienced in the here and now. Will I be still and know God's truth, forgiveness, and love, or keep running from myself? As I re-cover myself in God's hand each morning and evening many times a day, I must choose to honestly look at myself, face myself, forgive myself, and allow God to light my path.

Thy word is a lamp to my feet
and a light to my path.
Psalm 119: 105

Action: Go into a dark room and walk around for a few minutes. Did you stumble? Or, did you flip the switch to turn on the light. Notice how much easier, more comfortable, and safer it is to walk around when you can see.

Seeing life from God's view

An early morning walk by the lake reveals God's beautiful creation. The view changes with the seasons. As I walked during recent spring mornings, I witnessed how tough the winter had been on trees. Many branches had fallen to the ground—the usual twigs that the winter storms pruned from trees, and other large branches ripped off by the ravages of winter blizzards and the weight of heavy, icy rains. Some older trees fell over from the weight, while smaller trees were damaged by falling branches. Leaves, twigs, and trash had blown into the area or been dropped there by visitors. At times, it became difficult to walk through the mess. As I looked closer at some of the older, fallen trees, I could see the rings of its life. Each ring was different, impacted by the storms and availability of water (too little, too much, or polluted).

Much like the older, damaged trees, my own life has been ravaged. Like them, I've thrived at times. But I have suffered also and barely survived many seasons. Looking at the rings of my own life in God's Light of truth, I see the incredible ways He has used me when I was available to Him as one who was strong, of good courage, and thriving in His Living Water and seeking to do His Will, bearing good fruits in life, and sharing them with others.

I can see, also, times when I rushed along, believing I was doing His Will, but not taking the time to be with Him. It looked to the outward world as if I were doing a lot of good works and bearing fruit. In truth, my stressed fruit was not sweet: it dried and shriveled up, and dropped to the ground because it was not nourished with enough Living Water.

Trying to be more than I was, trying to be the best tree, always on the go, not seeing life in God's Light and sipping from the Living

Water less and less, I turned to polluted water (wine and other alcoholic spirits) to find relief from the constant demands of others and myself. I poisoned my life. Initially, there was enough strength in the years of good growth to handle this polluted water, but as my core became saturated, the damage became destructive and almost killed me (as well as others). Major branches of my life—including my love and passion for my family and my primary life's work—broke off causing damage to God, family, friends, co-workers, and my dreams.

As I see my life more clearly in God's Light, I can turn, run, hide, and return to the walking dead, or I can face my life one moment and one day at a time in God's loving forgiveness, forgive myself, live in His Light of truth, and drink from his well of Living Water.

Even though I walk through the valley of the shadow of death,
I will fear no evil;
for thou are with me;
thy rod and thy staff,
they comfort me.
Psalm 23:4

Action: Read Psalm 23. Take a walk in a woods or a park in a cluttered area, one that hasn't been cleared. Write about the clutter in your life, and how much easier it would be to move around if the clutter was removed.

Restoration

I have a beautiful, mature maple tree in my front yard—a resting spot for cardinals, chickadees, robins, and squirrels. Ducks, rabbits, a fox, and occasionally deer stop by (at times together) for corn, sunflower seeds, or bird food that I set out in a shaded area.

Several years ago, it was unclear if the tree would survive. When my parents planted the tree they routinely watered it, and the tree grew quickly. The majority of the soil, however, was sandy atop a layer of clay, which made it difficult for the tree to develop a deep root system. The roots became exposed more and more during a number of dry years, and I didn't take the time to water them.

After a few difficult winters, the maple cracked. Covering the damaged area kept the bugs from attacking it further, but only allowed it to survive, not thrive. The tree continued to struggle.

Later, a friend worked with me to clean out raunchy old leaves and junk, put a border around the tree, and cover the roots with a mulch mixture. Over the next few years, the tree's wounds began to heal, the tree's roots grew deeper, and the branches grew and filled—its beautiful gold and red leaves returned. The mulch had captured and kept close to its roots the living water it needed to grow and thrive.

There were times in my life when I was unsure if I would make it. The bandages of treatment weren't enough to help me thrive. I needed to humble myself, be willing to admit my faults, clean out raunchy old habits, remove stumbling blocks, and accept God's Living Water in order to be restored to the person He created me to be and to flourish. I had to take time to heal. My mulch became the ongoing re-covering in God of daily prayer, meditation, reading, and "being still" that allowed me to re-develop and grow deeper roots drinking deeply the living water. I also had to put up barriers by detaching from those people, places and things that were toxic and draining to me. These barriers allow the mulch to create a reservoir of living water to feed and heal my soul. I spend time with others who also want to be restored. Like trees in the forest together, we provide support and encouragement to each other by blocking stormy winds and providing shade for each other when feeling burnt out and weary.

> *If you knew the gift of God, and who it is that is*
> *saying it to you, 'Give me a drink,' you would have*
> *asked him, and he would give you living water.*
> **John 4:10**

Action: Identify and make a list of barriers that you need to create to protect yourself from toxic people, places, and situations. Identify ingredients of your mulch to create a reservoir of living water for your growth. Identify people and groups that you will mutually encourage and support your individual and collective restoration.

Damaged by the storms

Once when returning home after being out of town for a few days, I was saddened to find a major branch on my maple tree had cracked off from an ice and windstorm. The loss, especially in light of its earlier struggles, saddened me. The branch was on the side of the tree that had experienced most of the trauma from earlier storms.

After leaving it on the ground for a couple of days, I reluctantly went out one morning and pulled it away from the beautiful maple, which was beginning to bud out. Through the years I had watched as squirrels scampered up and down it, chickadees sat singing, and an occasional cardinal stopped by to rest on the branch. The branch would never experience any of this again.

The tree was damaged by freezing rain. I was damaged by frozen rage (a description often used by psychologists). Instead of dealing with anger and resentments when they surfaced, I shoved them aside, and they froze. When it thawed, as I was rushing through life trying to be more than I could, rather than deal with the anger and resentments, I drank. As a result, my frozen rage continued and I poisoned my life with alcohol. I could have allowed God's Light of truth to help me deal with the anger. I didn't. Consequently, I've lost several large branches. As those branches split off, it saddened and angered those who cared for me that I refused to take care of myself, that I didn't seek help earlier, and that I was unwilling to recognize the damage I was doing by maintaining the rage, workaholism, and alcohol poisoning.

After losing branches, I could leave my broken branches at the base of the tree, or I could deal with the consequences of my choices. Some of the branches I could move by myself. Others I needed help to clear away, which I've sought through fellowship in AA, an AA

Sponsor, and churches. While many of the dead branches have been cleared, the scars remain. I also must attend to those branches that landed on others, hurt them, and hurt their growth.

I dragged the maple tree branch to the side of the house, and later broke it up. Some of it would become mulch; some used to protect another tree, or help seedlings grow; some would be turned into kindling. An old Spanish proverb reads: " From a fallen tree, all make kindling."

Could and would God use my fallen branches for good? Will my re-covering in God and sharing his love and forgiveness, light a small fire, create a light for someone else to see some glimmer of hope, encourage another to want to learn to re-cover in God? It has become my prayer and hope!

For as the earth brings forth its shoots,
and as a garden causes what is sown in it to spring up,
so the Lord God will cause righteousness and praise
to spring forth before all the nations.
Isaiah 61:11

Action: Identify the branches in your life that have broken off. As you clear them away, write down how you will use those experiences to help others see the dangers of using a poison like alcohol to avoid issues in life?

Steadfast growth

Spring cleanup in my garden began with the removal of leaves I had placed on the flowerbed at the beginning of winter, which had protected the tulips from winter weather. As I moved the final covering of leaves and mulch, I smiled when I saw small sprouts of green growth: the flowers had survived.

During those first stormy days and months as the alcohol and prescription drugs left my body, friends and AA members covered and protected me with the mulch they had created from their own fallen branches—compassion developed as they addressed their own failures.

As I felt better and experienced God's presence and light, I grew quickly like the tulips in my garden. The first tulip that spring was a beautiful yellow one. I stopped and took pictures. I wanted more and more tulips to blossom. This is how I have often lived life—enjoying the beauty of God's creation for a brief moment, taking a picture to capture it, and then moving on and wanting to do more, instead of savoring the beauty of the moment.

The next tulip blossomed a week later—a gorgeous red and yellow one. I briefly looked at it and thought, "I'll take a picture when I get home," and rushed off to meetings. It was a dreadfully hot day—ninety-eight degrees. I came home, and the beautiful red and yellow tulip was bent over, drained by the extensive heat. I realized that I hadn't stopped to enjoy its beauty. I watered the tulip, and it recovered its blossoms. The tulip might never look as lovely as it had that beautiful moment early that spring morning, but the plant was saved, along with a chance for new blossoms next spring.

Much like my tulips, after each of my first two outpatient treatments, I blossomed quickly, then moved back into the heat of daily battles, expecting myself to do more and more without taking time to relax, enjoy life, and to be. It wasn't long before I was drained like the tulips. Instead of turning to Living Water, I turned to alcohol, which hurt me even more.

As I move through life re-covering in God, I am conscious of walking slower through life, pausing and being still, truly seeing the beauty of creation, wanting to walk with and not run ahead of God. Being steadfast in His love and living water gives me the opportunity to blossom each day.

Steadfast love and faithfulness will meet;
righteousness and peace will kiss each other.
Faithfulness will spring up from the ground,
and righteousness will look down from the sky.
Yea, the Lord will give us what is good
and our land will yield its increase.
Psalm 85:10–12

Action: Read Psalm 85. Go to a nursery and look at the flowers. Make a list of the blossoms in your life at this point in time.

Storm damages and clean up

I bought the home I grew up in as a child. The last few years have taken their toll on my yard and home with the accompanying storms, flash floods, and straight-line winds. During one particular storm, trees were brought down by the winds, and rushing water created a deep gulley along my fence; water poured into the basement.

I placed cement blocks into the gullies in order to redirect the water and stop the flooding of my basement. I hired workers to cut up the fallen trees. They created kindling and mulch from them. The yard has scars from the trees crashing down, and the damage done to the trees still standing continues to be visible.

During the last several years, I've created many of my own personal storms by an unwillingness to accept that I have the disease of alcoholism, a disease that will be with me for the rest of my life. By my refusal to accept this truth and ignoring the damage it was doing to my life, the consequences became progressively worse. I hurt many people and social justice causes that are important to me. As I clean up the damages from my personal storms, I must first take care of myself: spiritually, physically, intellectually, and emotionally. As I have re-covered each day in God, I have become willing to face the truth and consequences.

During the third week of treatment, I began to make a list of the people I had hurt, and specifically, the consequences of my behavior on them. I had damaged my witness as a person of faith. I had damaged relationships with family, friends, and co-workers through my denial, lies, actions and inaction. I asked God to guide me in his time as I sought to make amends to those I had harmed. As I was available to God, He gradually opened doors, slowly at first, and then more often as I began to engage more with the people and causes I had hurt. Making amends is very difficult: it is admitting the truth about my disease, how I ignored it, and how I have hurt others. It requires that I listen without making excuses or blaming anyone else, as they speak of the impact of my behavior on their lives. It requires that I apologize and demonstrate my sincerity by living a changed life.

> *O Lord who shall sojourn in Thy tent?*
> *Who shall dwell on Thy Holy Hill.*
> *He who walks blamelessly, and does what is right,*
> *and speaks the truth from his heart. . ..*
> **Psalm 15:1–2**

Action: Face the truth and make a list of all the people you have hurt. Decide to make amends to them. Ask God to guide you, in His time in making your amends with others.

Serenity

A portion of the serenity prayer written by Reinhold Niebuhr (circa 1943) is utilized at most AA meetings: "God grant me the serenity to accept the things I cannot change, the courage to change the things I can, and the wisdom to know the difference." I continue the prayer in my mind to paraphrase another portion of the prayer critical for me: Let your will, not my will, be done.

My experience in court profoundly impacted me. I had accepted a plea agreement admitting that I was guilty of driving under the influence and hurting two people. According to my attorney, I could have gone to trial, with the potential of having the case dismissed due to a mishandling of evidence and violation of my rights. As I prayed, I was certain that this was not God's Will. I chose to admit what was true: I was guilty, and I would face the consequences of my behavior.

Standing in court and listening to the brother and sister that I hurt describe the terror, physical injuries, and emotional trauma they experienced as my Jeep slammed into their vehicle at seventy miles per hour was painful. Fortunately, their elderly father escaped without injury. And yet, while the brother and sister were visibly and verbally angry with me, they also demonstrated compassion, a compassion stemming from their own pain, for their mother also had the disease—they understood this disease of alcoholism all too well.

Looking directly into their eyes, I broke down in tears as I expressed my sincere regret for my behavior. I admitted that I was wrong to drink while on prescribed medication and to drive while intoxicated. I told them I couldn't remember about an hour of my time driving or the accident. I apologized for hurting them. I let them know that I thanked God daily for protecting them from me. While this was incredibly difficult, their words became my memory of that day, and how dangerous I am when I allow alcohol to be in control.

I was fully aware that by pleading guilty, I would have a felony on my record, spend time in jail, and be on probation for six years. These were things I could not change. On the other hand, I could change my attitude. I could be available to God during incarceration and probation. In facing the truth and accepting the consequences of my actions, I was free to be, to love, care, reach out, be honest, and share my struggles and faith with others as I served my sentence.

Some of those I hurt choose not to be around me; some may never forgive me. I'm learning to accept each day that there are many things I cannot change.

I want to live life like a mountain stream that continues to flow, even around boulders and other obstacles. I pray that I may move through life with peace flowing in God's Will, having His wisdom to know His Will whether it is, No this cannot be changed now, the courage to change directions, or to wait for His timing.

If possible, so far as it depends upon you, live peaceably with all.
Romans 12:18

Action: Sit or walk by a river or a stream and watch as it moves around obstacles. Read the full serenity prayer and ask God for the wisdom to know what you can and cannot change, for courage, and for His Will to be done.

Reconstruction

Road construction and road repairs in Minnesota begin as soon as the snow melts and the ground thaws. The repairs may be as simple as filling in potholes on paved roads. Other roads may need to be re-surfaced with tar or gravel. Still others may be in such disrepair from years of neglect that a major breach in their foundation may require complete reconstruction.

With a complete road reconstruction, repairs begin with an inspection of the foundation. Next comes an assessment of the work needed, including a change of course for the road, if necessary, in order to address ongoing attacks to the foundation. Experienced road construction workers close the route, dig up and haul away the rubble and crumbled portions of foundation to be recycled into new pavement, pour a new foundation, and resurface with recycled pavement. Rumble strips are placed on the shoulder and centerline to alert drivers if they begin to drive off the path. To minimize the need for major repairs again, on-going maintenance of the road occurs.

My own path in life is not unlike this road repair ritual. Much of my life I've had a good foundation with God (thanks to my parents, Sunday School teachers, pastors, friends, prayer, meditation, journaling, the reading of God's Word and other devotionals). After many storms and wintery times, I've been able to make repairs by ridding my life of unhealthy behaviors or company and replacing them with healthier ones.

My first outpatient treatment and subsequent relapse treatment for alcoholism were attempts to repave my life, but I had failed to recognize and address the fact that I had a foundation cracking and disintegrating from years of workaholism, perfectionism, and alcohol use. At the same time, I hadn't continued to strengthen my base for life's journey.

During my first two outpatient treatments, I identified my perfectionism, workaholism, and some spiritual concerns. I refused to accept, however, that alcohol was toxic and destructive to my spiritual foundation. The re-pavement couldn't stand up to the elements when exposed to my daily schedule once again.

My life required more than a simple resurfacing. It required reconstruction. Closing the road, I admitted myself into Hazelden Treatment Center for seventy days of inpatient and on-site outpatient care. My life was dug up, the foundation inspected, and crumbled foundation identified. I wrestled with God on issues of faith, alcoholism, treatment methods, and sexist language used during this time of repairs. The old road in life was recycled and placed over my re-stored foundation. The new pavement, impressionable like hot tar, needed time to settle and firm up. Outpatient treatment aided in the solidification process.

I left Hazelden with a stronger foundation in God and renewed surface. Christian based individual therapy and an outpatient chemical health program assisted me in developing a new center and sidelines. Prayer, meditation, prayer journaling, walks in nature, church, Bible study, and AA serve as rumble strips and help me maintain a good, orderly direction and protect my foundation. In addition, I meet with a mentor or sponsor who has reconstructed her life, and other family and friends who love and have forgiven me.

Every one then who hears these words of mine and does them will be like a wise man who built his house upon the rock; and the rain fell, and floods came, and the winds blew and beat upon that house, but it did not fall, because it had been founded on the rock.
Matthew 7:24–25

Action: Go to a road construction site. Watch the process over next few weeks. Talk with a trusted friend about how you are reconstructing your life. Identify the rumble strips that help keep you on track.

Prayer

Prayer is often thought of as supplication—asking God for something. It may be blaming or cursing God for something we've done, like rushing and spilling coffee, shredding papers we meant to keep, hitting fingers with a hammer, or stubbing a toe. Each of the following is a prayer I've said to God at one time or another when I was drinking:

- ➤ God, I feel so awful, headache, throwing up, please let me feel better, I'll never drink again. God, why can't I stop drinking?
- ➤ I promise you, let things go my way and I'll stop drinking. I'll just drink today and God I promise I'll quit.
- ➤ God, please let me drive home safely and not get pulled over, I know I drank and shouldn't be driving.
- ➤ God, why did you let me get thrown in jail? God why have you abandoned me?

Jesus' disciples asked him to teach them to pray. He taught them a short, simple, yet profound prayer. In my own tradition, we pray: *Our Father, who art in heaven, hallowed be thy name. Thy Kingdom come, Thy Will be done, on earth as it is heaven. Give us today our daily bread; and forgive us our trespasses, as we forgive those who trespass against us; and lead us not into temptation, but deliver us from evil. For Thine is the Kingdom and Power and Glory forever. Amen.*

Wrestling with God I've learned this from the *Lord's Prayer* about the nature of prayer:

Our Father: God is everyone's God, a loving Father. Sadly, some have not had a loving dad like mine. If this is the case, you may need to find another example to help understand the nature of a loving father and child relationship.

Who art in heaven, Hallowed be thy Name. God is God, I am not. I am to honor that.

Thy kingdom come, Thy will be done on earth as it is in heaven: God wants us to live lives that share his love and reflect his light, so others can know his influence on our lives.

Give us today our daily bread: Asking God for the basic needs for today, not riches or to win the lottery, but rather, strength to live life well and in His presence, one day at a time.

Forgive us our trespasses as we forgive others. God forgives me of my wrongs when I ask him to do so. At the same time, when I pray this, I'm asking Him to limit the blessings of my experience of that forgiveness if I hold onto resentments or other things against someone else. As I forgive others, I'm free to be blessed with knowing the depth of God's forgiveness of me.

Lead us not into temptation; but deliver us from evil. I need to use the brain God gave me and be aware of what damages and destroys my foundation, and stay away from alcohol and unhelpful behaviors and situations. When situations arise for which I'm not prepared, I must ask God to show me how to get away from it, so that I am safe.

For Thine is the Kingdom and Power and Glory forever. For me, this is recognizing God is in charge and all powerful, and we are an heir to His Kingdom. I have wrestled with the word "glory" in the past and discovered that one definition is "the state of well being." Another way to look at it, then, is that I glorify God by being His person, by being a well-being. (Be In God)

Amen. "Amen" is defined as "so be it." In other words, the sentiments expressed in this prayer are to guide me in living my life.

Lord's Prayer: **Matthew 6:9–13**

Action: Pray this prayer daily for one week. Journal about the changes you've made in how you pray.

Prayer journaling

I've written in a prayer journal most of my adult life. As I look back on life, it's easy to identify the times when I have decreased or stopped taking time to sit, pray, and write: I live life my way, in my self-will again, instead of in God's Will. I run ahead, avoiding, ignoring or just plain refusing to do His Will. As I review past journals, it's clear that God and I have talked many times about my struggles with alcohol, and the poor choices and decisions I was making, but I refused to listen and accept that I was developing or had the disease called alcoholism.

Books on prayer journaling are readily available. I offer you my reasons for writing as a portion of my prayer time with God, as well as the format I follow.

I'm a very private, quiet, shy person in my personal life. I enjoy being alone. I share little with others, and when I do, I like to have thought through what I intend to say.

Writing helps me track my journey in life. As a psychologist I often said, awareness does not create change, change creates change. By being aware of my journey in life, I can work with God on plans to change my life, so I choose to change by being in His Will each day.

Writing is a slow process. It requires that I focus on one thought at a time. The process slows down my brain. I begin with dumping most things I'm thinking about onto paper—this includes my schedule, my worries, anger, hurts, disturbed and disgusted thoughts, struggles, undecided matters and concerns, and questioning of life. Writing gets it out of my head. Writing forces me to sit down and be in one place and take time to be. I begin to journal within the first 15–30 minutes after rising. I typically wake up full of energy, so I do a few morning chores, brew a cup of coffee, sit down, and write in my journal. The journal is a simple spiral notebook. The format I follow is a simple one:

1. I date the entry and start by writing, "Hi God."
2. Using free writing, I begin. It's a popular writing strategy that generally entails writing down everything that comes to mind with little or no editing—easy enough for me since this is just between me and God. (Of course, I recognize the inherent danger of journaling—someone may read it That said, I safeguard my journals, and my will requires them to be destroyed. Even so, there is always some concern in my head, and I'm not as blunt as my actual thoughts in order to protect others from being hurt, but also to protect myself.)
3. I jot down my schedule of the day, recognizing that God may interrupt or change it.
4. I read some devotionals and the Bible (the devotionals are listed in the Appendix).
5. I walk for twenty minutes or longer by a lake, a park, or in the woods, to release my physical energy and reflect on what I've read and seen in nature.
6. After returning from my walk, I sit by my fireplace and focus on the fire, quiet and still with God for 10–20 minutes.
7. I write what I sense God is saying to me through meditation, readings, and creation.

Therefore, I tell you, do not be anxious about your life,
what you shall eat, or what you shall drink, nor about your
body, what you shall put on. . . . [Y]our heavenly Father
knows you need them all. But seek first his kingdom and His
righteousness, and all these things shall be yours as well.
Matthew 6:25a, 32–33

Action: Prayer journal for a week. At the end of the week, write down 3–5 things you've discovered about yourself.

Meditation

I've mentioned earlier my love of long walks early in the morning as the sun rises, birds chirp, and geese and ducks lazily paddle in the lake by my home. It nurtures my spirit. The palette of colors, the smells of lilacs and wildflowers, and the sight of baby goslings and ducks exploring their new world while staying close to their moms— it all brings a smile to my face and joy to my heart. As I walk, I thank God for His Creation and the opportunity to enjoy it.

Early mornings also include a discipline of reading my Bible and devotionals, which stems from a desire to stimulate, challenge and engage my brain; to learn how others experience God, which may be unique, but also seems familiar.

Both the walks and the readings are ways in which I prepare for meditation.

Meditation is important in my life as it's a time I set aside to commune with God. Meditation is practiced and taught in various faiths such as Buddhism, and as a form of healthy living such as yoga, as well as through books and classes. Generally speaking, it's thought to be a time of quiet when one empties oneself of all thoughts.

Mediation for me is "to be still," or "cease striving." This is the process I use:

1. Writing down my concerns and thoughts in the prayer journal begins the process of emptying my mind.
2. After my walk, I return home, sit quietly, and gaze directly into the flames in my gas fireplace, or if it is too warm outside, I simply stare at the fireplace.

3. As thoughts come into my head, I choose not to entertain them; I let them go by repeating to myself, "Be still, and know I am God."
4. The amount of time varies each day, and it may take several minutes to reach the state of being still. While I set aside at least 15-20 minutes for meditations, at times I've found that a full hour has passed in communion with God.

It's my experience during meditation that God's Spirit is communing with the spirit He placed in me. That communion is beyond thought and sense. It is known only in the spiritual realm in the stillness and emptying of oneself. Sarah Young, in her devotional *Jesus Calling*, describes it as a "sacred space around you—space permeated with My [God's] Presence and My Peace" (Young 2004, 157).

After I complete this time of meditation, my mind often connects thoughts, readings, and experiences from the past and integrates them into different or new ways of thinking and seeing. I jot them down in my prayer journal. This may lead me back to the Bible or a devotional. In this way, it appears to me that God prepares and equips me with his insights and Word for the day.

For this reason I bow my knees before the Father, from whom every family in heaven and on earth is named that according to the riches of his glory he may grant you to be strengthened with might through his Spirit in the inner man, and that Christ may dwell in your hearts through faith; that you, being rooted and grounded in love, may have power to comprehend with all the saints what is the breath and length and height and depth, and to know the love of Christ which passes knowledge, that you may be filled with the fullness of God.
Ephesians 3:14–19

Action: Identify a quiet place: "be still." Meditate for ten minutes each day for a week.

Being aware

My maple tree survived and thrives—a great and beautiful tree, even with its scars and the loss of major branches. It's lush and full of leaves—a wonderful shade tree, and a place of safety for many animals and birds. From my picture window, I watch the cardinals, blue jays, wrens, and chickadees fly around and play in its branches.

Occasionally, a bird flies into my picture window. Most often, it flies away stunned but unharmed. Once in a while, it hits hard and falls onto the shrubs. If I witness the event, I check on the bird. Most often, upon seeing me, the bird flies off. Other times, the bird needs time to recover, so I move it to a safe place in the maple tree, which protects it from predators. The fact that the bird attempts flight again immediately and doesn't give up, strikes me as a natural response.

After this last alcoholic crash, I must be aware of the dangers that I may face as I begin to thrive, and I choose to fly again. The birds that hit my window, probably saw the reflection of trees and mistook the reflection for a tree itself. Those flying a little slower are able to veer off quickly. Those flying too fast smack against the window and are hurt in the process. My workaholism and perfectionism keep me in a frenzy as I attempt to get everything done. This sets me up for crashing into things I don't see coming. It prevents me from taking the time to take care of myself and remain attentive to how vulnerable I am at all times. I need to continue to learn to slow down, move at a steadier pace; as some would say, "Easy does it"; or a particular favorite, "God is not in a hurry, even if I am. He is always on time."

So, in addition to my morning time of prayer, walking, reading, meditation and reflection, I stop during the day simply to be still with God. And I'm making progress on taking time each night to sit and review my day. I ask God to help me see the progress I'm making, and to aide me in identifying dangerous people, places or things to my foundation; to look honestly at mistakes I've made and decide how I'll make amends. This honest evaluation of each day with God, let's me unburden my mind and sleep more peacefully.

I also call my AA sponsor or a friend when I hit something hard and feel hurt, upset, or damaged. I don't call expecting them to fix anything, but rather to listen to me, let me learn from it, and guide me in setting a plan to be safe as I take time to recover and persevere.

. . . [B]e strong in the Lord, and in the strength of His might. Put on the whole armor of God, that you may be able to stand against the wiles of the devil. . .. Pray at all times in the Spirit, with all prayer and supplication. To that end keep alert with all perseverance. . ..
Ephesians 6:10–11, 18

Action: Pray for God's guidance in obtaining an AA temporary sponsor or talking with a close sober friend about one area in your life that you seem to keep getting hurt by. Set up a plan to protect and take care of yourself.

New directions

As a child, we took family trips to National Parks. Trips to the Rocky Mountains were my favorite. I often daydreamed (and still do) of living in a small cabin in the foothills of the mountains with the summits covered with snow. I imagined in front of the cabin, down a slight hill, a mountain stream, pine trees, wild flowers, green grass, deer, birds, and mountain goats; of watching the sunrise through the foothills and glorious sunsets between the mountain ranges; of inviting friends to visit and enjoy God's beautiful creation. From my experience of hiking several mountain ranges, I was aware that creeks that developed from snow melting and rain fed into the mountain streams, and sometimes, when heavy rains or snow came it caused flooding, landslides, and avalanches. In my daydreams, I developed plans to protect my cabin by creating dams and re-directing creeks.

As I move on in life, accepting alcoholism as a disease, this dream regularly surfaces. It symbolizes my love of nature and God's creation, and a desire to re-build my life in a place of serenity where I can be at peace with God, myself, and others.

Just as I was aware as a child of the potential for weather that would out be out of my control, I'm aware now that there will be events in life that I can't control: I call these Activating Events. Over the years I've developed patterns of how I deal with such events—some are healthy, others are not and have often led me back to drinking. Those patterns, like the small creeks, have become engrained, as are my beliefs about that event, which may or may not be accurate. Unless I change my behaviors and beliefs, the consequences will damage or destroy me.

I choose to build dams in order to protect myself. I utilize prayer, my AA Sponsor, AA, Church, close friends, and walking in nature as a part of my dam system.

Dams, however, break when under too much pressure and greater damage can be done. So in addition to the dams, I must create new beliefs and redirect my thoughts in healthier patterns. When I talk through my old thinking with others, I can set a new direction and have my beliefs and thoughts about the event move into a new and healthier direction. Old patterns begin to fade, though they will never disappear, and they'll always take me down the path of destruction if I don't redirect and create a new, safer path for my life.

As difficult events occur in life, a quick way to remember this is A, B, C, D, E:

Activating Event: A harsh word, an unexpected outcome, any event that causes distress

Belief: What am I thinking—it is healthy or not?

Consequences: What are the consequences of heading down this path with unhealthy thinking?

Dam: Disputing those beliefs or thoughts through prayer and reaching out to others for support. Dreaming again and moving in new spiritual directions.

Enjoying: Serenity, peace with God, myself, and others

If I don't do this, my **D** becomes "Damn it, I don't care," which leads to Drinking and Drowning my thoughts and feelings—Destructive attitudes and behaviors.

My **E** becomes "Escape" from my thoughts and feelings through alcohol, which destroys me, others, my relationship with God; it will "End" my life.

Do not lie to one another, seeing that you have put off the old nature with its practices and have put on the new nature, which is being renewed in knowledge after the image of its creator.
Colossians 3: 9–10

Action: Read Colossians 3:5–17. Identify patterns you need to change, dams you need to build, and new directions to develop. Share it with another person.

Growing strong and being fruitful

Clearing out the leaves in my backyard garden one day, I discovered a maple sapling growing—perhaps an offspring of the old maple tree in my front yard. I stepped around to the front of the house to look at the tree, it buds having developed into glorious large green leaves after the healthy spring rains. On the trunk, visible scars from where branches were wrenched away. Yet, as I step back to view the entire tree, it's magnificent—tall and strong with branches like outstretched arms providing cover and a cool resting place.

As I continue to pray and meditate daily, my roots grow deep in God's spiritual foundation. No longer poisoning my life with alcohol and the insanity such spirits brought into my life, I can grow again and thrive, instead of simply survive or die.

As storms come, which they will, as I choose to drink God's Living Water, I will be strong in Him; I will not only weather the storms but increase in strength.

Although I've been damaged by storms, both those which I had no control over and those that I created by poor choices, I can blossom again and be covered in the goodness of God's grace I will glorify Him by being well. My life can continue to reproduce His good fruit as I abide in God's Spirit, the fruits of love: joy, peace, patience, kindness, goodness, faithfulness, gentleness, and self-control.

I will share these good fruits. I will share what God has taught me with others. Like seeds being scattered, the ones that land on good soil like my sapling maple tree will take root and grow. We each have a choice about our willingness to accept God's Will for our lives. Your life can be a hardened path. The alcohol spirits may keep you from knowing God, or keep you from developing roots in him. You can be so busy that cares, riches, and the pleasures of life keep you from growing and developing strong roots. Or, you can be open to being held close in God's Spirit with an honest and good heart and allow God's Spirit to grow in you and bring fruit in His timing.

[Jesus tells this parable.] *The seed is the word of God. The ones along the path are those who have heard; then the devil comes and takes away the word from their hearts, that they may not believe and be saved. And the ones on the rock are those who, when they hear the word, receive it with joy; but these have no root, they believe for a while and in time of temptation they fall away. And as for what fell among the thorns, they are those who hear, but as they go on their way they are choked by the cares and riches and pleasures of life, and their fruit does not mature. And as for that in the good soil, they are those who, hearing the word, hold it fast in an honest and good heart, and bring forth fruit with patience.*
Luke 8:11–15

Action: Buy some seeds. Scatter them on a road, rocks, or mixed in thistles. Scatter others in good black soil. Watch these seeds over the next month. Write down what you need to do to open your heart, soul, mind, and strength to God's Word.

Scars and character

In my pre-teen years, my chemistry set played a large part in my life. In high school, others routinely turned to me in chemistry class for help. One particular experiment comes to mind: we sought to heat a substance and transform it from a liquid to a solid with little success. Determined to succeed, I heated the substance till the test tube exploded. Hot chemicals sprayed onto my hand and face. Without safety glasses, I'd have been blinded. My face had small burns, and my left hand was burned severely. Bandages and a plastic bag covered my hand for weeks. Doctors were adamant: keep it covered and let it heal gradually; otherwise, it wouldn't heal well, and the scars would become more pronounced. I diligently cared for my wounds. When asked about the faded scars, I share this story to encourage others to take care of themselves, to avoid being stubborn and reckless as was I, and to let themselves heal properly when hurt.

As an adult, I played with alcohol. Initially it was fun. Eventually I used it as an escape. As I worked harder and harder to prove that I knew how to solve homelessness in our nation, I drank more and more to avoid the emotional pain of seeing people without homes, and to cope with the lack of compassion, equity, and justice for them in this society.

Exercise is a healthy way to deal with such stress, especially when compared to drinking; but in my last relapse, I hurt my body by over exercising. Doctors prescribed pain medications, which complicated matters. Unwilling to see that what I was doing wasn't working and ask for help, I imploded: I drank, hurt myself, others, and scarred my life's work.

As I heal, I live more consistently in God's Will. In reconstructing portions of my foundation, I've reordered my thoughts and priorities as I more fully understand God's Order from the Scriptures. My life had many dis-orders: things I had been taught, experienced, and faulty thinking created when trying to manage on my own. As I understand God's Order more and more, I don't view it as Him ordering me around, but rather how He created me and ordered the healthiest way to live life.

I listen to my body. When it's tired and hungry, I rest and feed it healthy food. When I feel angry, hurt, or upset, instead of dulling the pain with alcohol, I stop and be still with God; or, if there's too much energy, discharge it by exercising, crying, screaming alone in my home, or, talking with someone till I can settle down and hear what God wants me to learn.

Feelings are helpful: like sitting by a fire, they can be warm and comfortable. At other times, they can tell me I'm in danger of being burnt. I call this healthy guilt, when my feelings alert me that I'm doing something wrong. I don't need to shame myself. I can't know everything. Nor must I tolerate or stay in a situation until I get burnt or explode. Feelings offer important pieces of information. Yet, they are horrible decision makers; that's my head's job. Only when sober and in God's Order will I make healthy decisions.

Scars remain from the past. I can repeatedly reopen them, stare at them, and refuse to let them heal properly. Alternatively, I can let them heal and scar over, let my character grow in God's Order, and not be afraid to learn from them or allow others see them healing and learn from my experiences.

Be watchful, stand firm in your faith, be courageous,
be strong. Let all that you do be done in love.
I Corinthians 16:13–14

Action: The next time you receive a small cut or bruise, watch how it heals. Do you generally tell others about some of your physical aches and pains? List the reasons you're afraid to show your scars from alcoholism.

Priorities

I'm amazed at how often I smile, laugh, and joke with others these days. I sense a growing peace within myself, about myself, and in sharing myself with others.

When I began thinking about writing this devotional, I was hesitant to tell many what the devotional was about, clearly embarrassed about this disease of alcoholism. Over the last few months as I have continued to heal in God's love, accept and love myself more, I am less afraid to share my story and struggle with alcoholism.

I've also noticed a significant change in my view of Re-Covering in God. Initially, the metaphor that came to me was the image of my small hand forming a fist, which I then placed into my larger hand. I then closed my larger hand, covering the smaller one, like a refuge protecting me from everything and everyone, but especially from the grips of the spirits of alcoholism, workaholism, and perfectionism.

As I continued to wrestle with God and the writing of this devotional, the image changed: my fist began to open up, like a bud on a tree, as I experienced God's Light, love and warmth. My life is less closed off, and I am no longer hiding. My spirit has begun to blossom again. I'm no longer afraid to be held in God's open Hand, and to enjoy His Peace, Light and Order.

As I continually choose to re-order life and reconstruct my foundation based on God's Order and Foundation, I'm moving into a new stage of re-covering. I'm re-covering the specialness of the me that God created me to be. God's love for me has given me the courage to love myself and life again. I love walking and talking with God about His Order and Will. It's as if our fingers intertwine hand in hand, and we swing our arms, sometimes walking, running, or sitting still with each other. It's amazing and incredible to be in His Presence, Love and Peace.

As we hold hands and walk together, He reminds me I can always run to Him and seek refuge in Him when I'm clenched in pain, anger, hurt, or afraid of other spirits. He will protect me and show me a way out. He will have time to walk, play, talk, listen, wrestle, love and enjoy His creation with me. Yet, He is clear there is more to life.

The Holy Scriptures tell me that God's priorities for human beings are:

1. To love God with all my heart, soul and mind;
2. To love others as myself.

Finding that balance is the struggle that God and I will continue to wrestle with. Far too often my desire is to jump ahead and take care of something for someone else, without talking and listening to know what God or what others want. That jumping ahead has hurt others by disrespecting their abilities and not allowing them to learn to take care of things themselves; by giving and doing more than I can or should, thereby hurting myself.

> *And [Jesus] said . . . "[Y]ou shall love the Lord your God with all your heart, with all your soul, and with all your mind. This is the great and first commandment. And a second is like it, You shall love your neighbor as yourself. On these two commandments depend all the law and the prophets."*
> **Matthew 22: 37–40**

Action: Go to a playground with a friend and play on a teeter-totter.

Life is a balancing act

The teeter-totter is a piece of playground equipment that requires us to have someone else to play with us in order for it to function properly. We can sit on one end hitting the ground, of course, or prop ourselves up, pretending to be balanced with our feet on the ground. We can even jump up to get the feel of playing. Nonetheless, it requires another person on the other side to enjoy fully this simple piece of playground equipment. With the other, we can go up and down, or try to adjust so that we are both balanced without having our feet touch the ground. There's little fun to be had when someone always wants to be up, or the other is always down, and it hurts when one jumps off and the other crashes to the ground. Both crash to the ground if the board disengages from the fulcrum (the pivotal point).

We live in a culture that preaches and glorifies self-sufficiency, self-reliance, self-righteousness, self-fulfillment, self-gratification, self-seeking, self-sacrifice, self-satisfaction, do-my-own-thing, pulling myself by my bootstraps. It's all about self.

At the same time, many of us are lonely. We seek distractions from daily monotony, pain and suffering, with distractions such as alcohol. We don't know how to get along or play together, because we lack or underutilize a strong base that provides the pivotal point for all our interactions with ourselves and others.

The teeter-totter provides a clear illustration of how we might view God's priorities and how to enjoy life. The base (pivotal point) is faith in Jesus, and we sit on one side of the teeter-totter; others sit on the opposite side. As long as I base my life on Jesus, I have the opportunity to live in peace and harmony with others by loving and treating others the way I want to be treated. We can play together in life, each taking turns, never keeping track of the number of times we help each other as we go up and down. We can adjust where we sit to see if we can be equally balanced even though we are very different, knowing we can't do it alone, and neither can they; knowing you can't do their role, nor can they do yours. This is interdependence; it is how, I believe, we as humans were created to be with God.

To en-JOY life. I must live within how God has ordered life: To love God and love others as myself.

JOY =   Jesus   Others   You

Others_____You

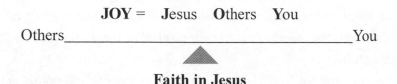

Faith in Jesus

> *. . . [L]ead a life worthy of the calling to which you have been called, with all lowliness and meekness, with patience, forbearing one another in love, eager to maintain the unity of the Spirit in the bond of peace.*
> **Ephesians 4:1–3**

Action: Play on the teeter-totter with a friend. Adjust yourselves to be in balance. Let one be up and then the other. Watch how the pivot point is always the center of the movement. Write how you will create a more balanced life.

Together

Watching a flock of geese fly is an incredible sight. They fly together for great distances in a V formation, each taking turns as they rotate to the front to lead and break the wind for the others. They adjust their V in strong winds in order to maximize their energies in their flight pattern.

Geese mate for life. They are very protective of their young. They are loyal to each other within the flock. When one goose struggles or is hurt and can't continue to fly with the flock, one or two geese will drop out of the flock to be with the hurt goose until it heals and can fly again, or until it passes away.

The geese sense when it's time to head north to their usual nesting areas. After raising their young, protecting them from dangers, teaching them to fly, most will fly south to avoid being caught in dangerous wintery storms.

As human beings we can learn from geese: how to move through life taking turns in both leading and following; how to help each other working together and sharing our journey; loyalty and dedication to each other in our relationships; how to love and protect our children, teach them how to live in common unity, sharing the load and caring for each other.

The disease of alcoholism paralyzed me, and I was unable to continue my journey in life. Most continued on with their lives, but others dropped some of the things they were doing to be with me as I sought healing through treatment. They couldn't fix me. They knew I had to find The Way to heal if I was to "fly" again. As I completed treatment, I found others who would support me as I learned to live life without alcohol—people who knew first-hand the suffering that comes with this disease of alcoholism and were able to walk with me in my suffering and healing as others had walked with them in their time of great need. This is true compassion—being in suffering with another person. Being with them, not trying to fix, correct, judge, or take care of them, but being with them and allowing God to use you and let His miracle of faith, hope and love touch those suffering.

I want to live in common unity with others. I want to share the compassion shown me by being available to God to be with others in their suffering, to be His woman, available to let others know of His faithfulness, hope, forgiveness and love as they heal from alcoholism, tragedies, struggles, diseases, or in their last years in life.

So faith, hope, and love abide, these three;
but the greatest of these is love.
I Corinthians 13:13

Action: Thank the people who have been with you during this time of suffering for their compassion. Share with them how you will be compassionate toward others.

A life of love

I Corinthians 13 has long been one of my favorite chapters in the Bible. Many know it as the "Love Chapter." The middle verses are often quoted in marriage ceremonies. Unfortunately, the beginning and ending of the chapter receive less attention. In my opinion, these verses are key to being and living in God's love.

A good portion of my life has been spent going and doing: self-sacrificing, controlling, giving advice, trying to change the world, too often in my own power and not in God's love. I was, as described in the first few verses of the chapter, like a noisy gong, clanging cymbal, giving away resources, and much of myself. When it was not done in God's love, I saw little or no gain. Over the last few years, I've turned to alcohol spirits for relief from the wasted efforts instead of recognizing that only in God's spirit of love would life be meaningful.

In God's Spirit, "Love is patient and kind; love is not jealous or boastful; it is not arrogant or rude. Love does not insist on its own way; it is not irritable or resentful; it does not rejoice at wrong, but rejoices in right. Love bears all things, believes all things, hopes all things, endures all things" (vv. 4-7). It's helpful for me to remember, that in order for me to love unconditionally, I must be connected and re-covered in God's love each moment of the day. I can't love unconditionally on my own, or when controlled by any other spirit—only in God's Spirit.

"Love never ends" (v. 8a): people have loved and encouraged me unconditionally. What a difference that has made in my life! In addition, I'm aware of how others have been impacted when I've been available for God's Love to flow through me. I don't want to invest the time left to me on earth accumulating material things. My achievements, in the scheme of eternity, will have little significance without love. I want to reflect God's Light, utilize my storm damaged branches as kindling for starting new fire in others; to be mulch that protects new saplings from the weeds that can entangle them; to help others find and drink from the Living Water so that they, too, can thrive instead of continuing to drink from the poison that alcohol has been in our lives.

To live a life of faith, hope, and love gives meaning to these brief moments of being on this planet. Being in God and available to allow His Love flow to me and through me is the key to being fully alive.

While I have seen and known glimpses of this love throughout my life, I know and understand it more and more each day as I am re-covered in His Spirit. As I continue this journey, one step at a time, I believe God will continue to reveal himself, and I will reflect His Light and Love more and more each day: "For now we see in the mirror dimly, but then face to face. Now I know in part; then I shall understand fully, even as I have been fully understood. Faith hope, and love abide and the greatest of these is love." (I Corinthians 13:12,13)

Therefore be imitators of God, as beloved children.
And walk in love, as Christ loved us. . ..
Ephesians 5:1–2a.

Action: Read and memorize I Corinthians 13.

A Creative Work in Progress

Just as a journey begins with a single step, the transformation of our lives will occur one day at a time, as we make the choice to be in God's will instead of our self-will.

Mother Theresa tells us in *A Gift for God,* "Faith is lacking because there is so much selfishness and so much gain for self. But faith, to be true, has to be a giving love. Love and faith go together. They complete each other" (New York: HarperCollins, 1996, 16). As I have faith in God to transform me, He helps me to better love Him, myself and others. I find joy and peace in and with the world when I love God with my heart, soul, mind and all my strength, and I love others as I love myself.

As new opportunities avail themselves, I want "to lead a life worthy of the Lord, fully pleasing to Him, bearing fruit in every good work and increasing in the knowledge of God (Col. 1:10–11).

It wasn't easy for me to look back at the terrible mistakes I've made on my journey in life and the major flaws in my tapestry of life. But I can choose to focus on that or on where God is leading me now. At the same time, I'm keenly aware of my own fears of being successful again, and the dangers of thinking that I did it on my own, and of becoming boastful of any accomplishments instead of giving all glory to God working through me.

I know that I can do nothing. God can do everything. O God, make me Thy fit instrument and use as thou wilt! (Gandhi Young India, 1924). As I move along this journey of re-covering in God each day, I want to be available to Him to do His will. I must not focus on past failures, but learn from them, stop procrastinating, and be open to new challenges and opportunities, recognizing my control is only in my choice to do His will not in the outcomes.

Marianne Williamson's meditation on human fears often surfaces as I make my way through the day:

Our deepest fear is not that we are inadequate,
Our deepest fear is that we are powerful beyond measure.
It is our light, not our darkness, that most frightens us.
We ask ourselves, who am I to be brilliant,
gorgeous, talented, fabulous?
Actually who are you <u>not</u> to be? You are a child of God.
Your playing small doesn't serve the world.
There is nothing enlightened about shrinking so others people
Won't feel insecure around you.
We were born to make manifest the glory of God that is within us.
It is not just in some of us; it's in every one of us. And as we let
Our own light shine, we unconsciously
give other people permission to
do the same. As we are liberated from our own fear,
our presence automatically liberates others.
(Williamson 1992, 190–91).

It is my hope and prayer as we each continue to re-cover in God, grow in our love for God and ourselves that we may be a light for others as we share our struggles, compassion, hope, faith, love. My prayer is that we will choose to be re-covered in God and we be in what God is creating and blessing each day.

Appendix: Resources

Material is listed in the order in which I drew upon most heavily in developing this devotional. Those materials published specifically for Alcoholics Anonymous and Al-anon are listed separately.

Holy Bible Revised Standard Version Harper Study Bible. 1976. Grand Rapids: Zondervan Publishing House.

"Pleasure Unwoven." 2009. Kevin McCauley, M.D. DVD. Salt Lake City: Institute for Addiction Study.

Young, Sarah. 2004. *Jesus Calling: Enjoying Peace in His Presence*. Nashville: Thomas Nelson.

Mansfield, Stephen. 2012. *Lincoln's Battles with God*. Nashville: Thomas Nelson.

Warren, Rick. 2003. *The Purpose Driven Life*. Philadelphia: Running Press.

Powell, John. 1976. *Fully Human, Fully Alive*. Niles, Illinois: Argus Communication.

Niebuhr, Reinhold. Circa 1941. "The Serenity Prayer" as quoted in *The Serenity Prayer*. Elisabeth Sifton. 2005. New York: W. W. Norton.

Mother Theresa. 1996. *A Gift for God*. New York: HarperCollins Paperback.

Rubin, Sergio and Amborogetti, Francesca. 2013. *Pope Francis Conversations with Jorge Bergoglio*. New York: G.P. Putnam's Sons.

Mohandas Gandhi. 1922. Quote from "Young India." Mani Bhavan Gandhi Sangrahalaya, "My Faith." Gandhi Philosophy. http://www.gandhi-manibhavan.org/gandhiphilosophy/philosophy truth truthisgod.htm.

Enger, David. 1982. *Praying with Confidence*. Grand Rapids: Discovery House Publishers.

Roper, David. 2000. *Growing Slowly Wise: Building a Faith That Works*. Grand Rapids: Discovery House.

Crowder, Bill. 2012. *Moving Beyond Failure: Lessons from Peter*. Grand Rapids: Discovery House.

Bower, Christy. 2010. *Best Friends with God: Falling in Love with the God Who Loves You*. Grand Rapids: Discovery House.

Chambers, Oswald. 2012. *If you will ask: Reflections on the Power of Prayer*. Grand Rapids: Discovery House.

Kendall, R.T. 2004. *Total Forgiveness Experience: A Study Guide to Repairing Relationships*. Lake Mary, Florida: Charisma House.

Our Daily Bread. 2012–13. Grand Rapids: RBC Ministries.

Chittister, Joan D. 1996. *The Psalms Meditations For Every Day of the Year*. New York: Crossroad Publishing.

Williamson, Marianne. 1992. *A Return to Love: Reflections on the Principles of "A Course in Miracles."* HarperOne.

Alcoholics Anonymous and Al-anon Books

Twenty-Four Hours A Day. 1975. Daytona Beach: Hazelden Foundation.

Courage to Change. 1992. Virginia Beach: Al-Anon Family Group Headquarters, Inc.

Twelve Steps and Twelve Traditions. 2011. New York City: Alcoholics Anonymous World Services, Inc.

Drop the Rock Removing Character Defects. 2005. Center City, Minnesota: Hazelden Foundation.

About the Author

Sue Watlov Phillips is a woman of God who seeks to serve faithfully the Lord through her passion of social justice by serving people experiencing homelessness or housing crisis, and people with chemical, mental, and physical health issues. She drank alcohol normally for 25 years. After menopause, alcohol began to impact her life in a negative manner. After struggling with alcohol for 7 years during which she almost lost her relationship with God, family, friends and her life, Sue placed herself in an in-patient treatment center. This devotional is the outgrowth of her on-going wrestling with God over alcoholism, workaholism, athleticism, perfectionism, and other –isms, her determination to understand more fully the nature of recovery, and her struggle to re-cover in God each day.

With a B. A. in Psychology and M. A. in Counseling and Psychological Services, she is a retired Licensed Psychologist, Independent Clinical Social Worker, Marriage and Family Therapist and Certified Sports Psychologist.

Sue has worked for 44 years in social justice, with an emphasis on serving people experiencing homelessness or in a housing crisis, she developed some of the first transitional housing, prevention, and rapid rehousing models in the country (Elim Transitional Housing, Inc.), in the early 1980s, which became a model for local, state and federal legislation. Throughout the last 4 decades she has also contributed to the writing of Minnesota and Federal legislation regarding mortgage foreclosure prevention, affordable housing, livable incomes, affordable health care and transit, excellence in education and job training, protection of our environment and protecting and honoring people's civil rights. She is the Owner, President and CEO of Integrated

Community Solutions, Inc., a for profit consulting company. Sue currently serves as the interim Executive Director of the Metropolitan Interfaith Council on Affordable Housing- MICAH. As a Founding Board Member, she has provided this service to MICAH 4 four times during MICAH's 26 years of advocating for affordable housing in the Twin Cities community. As a consultant, teacher, and writer, she often speaks at workshops, conferences, teaches Bible Studies. She is co-author of several publications including Rapid *Re-Housing Manual* (2010), *Foreclosure to Homelessness* (2008 and 2009), and a contributor to *Without Housing* (2010). She served on the Advisory Committee (2013-14) as a co-author of Adapting Clinical Practice for the Care of Homeless Patients with Opioid Use Disorders (March 2014) for the Health for the Homeless Clinician's Network.

Sue bought the home she grew up in and lives with her cat in Fridley, Minnesota. On the weekends, she helps a friend manage a resort in northern Minnesota. She visits her mother in assisted living, where she also facilitates Bible Studies and serves as a substitute pastor.